MW01096920

THE Mangalitsa Pig

ROYALTY
IS COMING TO AMERICA

Sok Szeretettel

S안ály

26.05.2019.
Budahely...

**A History of the world famous breed featuring illustrated
recipes by top Hungarian chefs and restaurants**

© ALL RIGHTS RESERVED.
Without limiting the rights under copyright reserved above, no part of this publication may be reproduced,
stored in or introduced in to a retrieval system, or transmitted, in any form or by any means (electronic, mechanical,
photocopying, recording or otherwise), without the prior written permission of the copyright owner
and the above publisher of the book. The content of the book is subject to alteration without notice.

PUBLISHED BY BOOOK PUBLISHING HUNGARY 2014
Web: www.boook.hu | Facebook: www.facebook.hu/Boook | Email: info@boook.hu

CONCEPT AND ART WORK: BOOOK PUBLISHING

AUTHORS OF THE MANGALITSA CONNECTION: BARBARA MEYER ZU ALTENSCHILDESCHE , WILHELM W. KOHL
AUTHOR OF THE INTRODUCTION: WILHELM W. KOHL
AUTHOR OF THE HISTORY OF THE MANGALITSA: PÉTER TÓTH
THE TEXT WAS LEAD AND EDITED BY JASON B. KOHL

COVER ILLUSTRATION: MÁTÉ DOBESCH
PROFESSIONAL SUPERVISION: LÁSZLÓ RUPRECHT CHEF, TAMÁS BEREZNAY CHEF

PHOTOS
RESTAURANTS, FOOD AND LIFESTYLE: BALÁZS GLÓDI
FOOD STYLIST: ÁRON BARÁTH

ARCHIVE PHOTOS:
HUNGARIAN NATIONAL ASSOCIATION OF MANGALITSA BREEDERS, FORTEPAN
PAGE 5, 7, 8: DÁNIEL VÉGEL | PAGE 12, 23, 24: ANKE RIJKSEN | PAGE 13, 14: JAN MARIE EVANS
PAGE 15: PEARL THE MANGALITSA: KATE MOUNTAIN, LODGE AND FARM
PAGE 26-27 /MEAT PHOTOS : TONY INCONTRO, NAPA VALLEY

GRAPHIC DESIGN AND ART WORK: KRISZTA KLEBERCZ

PROOFREADERS: LILLA CSÁK, MÁRTON BALLA
TRANSLATOR: ESZTER SZALAI
EDITOR: BEÁTA BENCSICS
EDITORIAL DIRECTOR: VIKTOR BALÁZS
PRODUCER: PÉTER SZÉPLAKI

In the first edition Judit Osvárt and Dávid Baráth were collaborating.

SUPPORTERS:

  PUREmangalitsa

Special thanks to Barbara Meyer zu Altenschildesche, Péter Tóth, Wilhelm W. Kohl, Marc Santucci, Anke Rijksen, Jan Marie Evans,
Kate Mountain, Jason B. Kohl, Tony Incontro, Dániel Végel and for all fans of the Mangalitsa Pig !
Special thanks for the support of the Hungarian National Association of Mangalitsa Breeders www.mangalicatenyesztok.hu !
Thanks to the chefs and restaurants' owners for their cooperation in compiling this book !

Made in Keskeny Press, 2014, ISBN 978-615-5417-04-7 The Mangalitsa, Boook Kiadó

CONTENT

INTRODUCTION

THE MANGALITSA PIG IN AMERICA

WRITTEN BY : WILHELM W. KOHL

Back then I knew little about pigs. I knew they were the most popular meat in Europe. As an Austrian I also knew that cooking with lard tastes infinitely better than butter, olive oil, or just about anything else. I learned my love of lard from my Austrian mother, who never skimped on it in her home cooking, which is still the best food I've ever tasted.

This is what went through my mind as I stared at the wooly pig in front of me. Little did I know that the first Mangalitsa pig had already arrived in the United States.

In 2007 Heath Putnam, a Seattle-based entrepreneur, was the first person to import Mangalitsa pigs from Austria. Putnam wanted a tastier pork, and the Mangalitsa did not disappoint.

Unlike most gene-tweaked American pigs, the Mangalitsa's genetics have remained untouched since the breed's creation in 1833, when some unknown genius first bred the Mangalitsa for an Archduke in the Austro-Hungarian Empire.

The Mangalitsa was bred to produce two things; exquisitely marbled meat and pure white fat. It was so successful on both fronts that within 20 years Mangalitsa became the dominant Central European breed.

I stared in disbelief at what looked like a practical joke: a pig covered in wool. I was in Sebersdorf, a tiny Austrian village near Graz, the capitol of Styria. My friend pointed at the strange beast – "I don't know what breed they are, but they're the best damn pig I ever tasted," he said.

That was how I met the Mangalitsa.

The pigs' success came from its lard, which is beyond anything I've ever tasted. At the time of this writing, Mangalitsa lard is only available in America through a handful of specialty retailers, but that is bound to change. The stuff is like crack cocaine for foodies.

The lard was also an extremely valuable source of calories for Austria-Hungary's growing population. Mangalitsa lard fueled Austria-Hungary's industrial revolution, and led to the first large-scale hog production in human history.

The Mangalitsa even inspired its own Operetta. In 1885 Johann Strauss wrote "The Gypsy Baron," wherein a wealthy pig farmer declares

> Ja, das Schreiben und das Lesen
> Ist nie mein Fach gewesen,
> Denn schon von Kindesbeinen
> Befaßt ich mich mit Schweinen,
>
> Auch war ich nie ein Dichter
> Potz Donnerwetter Parapluie!
> Nur immer Scheinezüchter
> Poetisch war ich nie!

> *I've no time for learning writing,*
> *breeding pigs is too exciting*
> *and I've got no time for reading,*
> *for the pigs will keep on breeding*
>
> *So I've never been a reader,*
> *for reading I don't care two figs,*
> *I'm just a humble breeder,*
> *who keeps on breeding pigs*

When a man chooses pigs over literacy you know you've got some powerful lard!

The Mangalitsa remained a fixture of fine dining until 1945, when Hungary came under Communist rule. Suddenly eating out became so expensive that only high Communist officials and foreign businessmen could enjoy it. Tragically, Hungary's great culinary tradition thus entered a 40 year slumber.

But after the fall of the Iron Curtain in 1989, the situation changed rapidly. New businesses opened, tourism exploded, and the Hungarian culinary tradition was reborn. Famous Hungarian wines like "Tokaji" and "Bull's Blood" returned to the sclerotic veins of Hungarian cooking schools, along with the beloved Mangalitsa.

There are now hundreds of great restaurants in Budapest alone, many of which serve the Mangalitsa of Hungary's golden years. Just take a look at this Mangalitsa loin and you'll understand this pig's tremendous potential for American kitchens.

It's already in America's top restaurants. The Mangalitsa began its takeover of American fine dining in late 2007 when Putnam shipped pork to the French Laundry, a renowned restaurant in Yountville, California. It hasn't left Chef Thomas Keller's menu since.

And then of course you can enjoy three week aged Mangalitsa pork loin, with grilled abalone, at Atera in New York, a Four Star Restaurant for 2014.

The reason why is simple; as a traditional, unmodified breed, Mangalitsa is the opposite of most American pork, which is bred for rapid growth and lean meat. Unlike "the other white meat," Mangalitsa is deep red in color, closer to beef than whatever passes for pork these days. The Mangalitsa's soft fat tastes more like cream or butter, again unlike the pork fat most Americans so diligently slice away from their pork chops.

Sam Hazen, Executive Chef at Veritas in New York, knows how special the Mangalitsa meat is. After using it for several years he says that "It's the best pork in the world. It's got incredible texture and it's consistent; it's never dry. It's very, very special." [1]

I'm equally convinced that the Mangalitsa will transform 21st century American cooking. 10 years ago how many Americans had ever tasted Lardo, or even knew what Charcuterie was? How many Americans had knowingly eaten pure fat? Or have even considered it?

Mario Batali, a renowned expert on Italian cuisine, was one of the first great American chefs to serve Lardo; "At the restaurant, I tell the waiters to call it Prosciutto Bianco"[2] Soon after "Prosciutto Bianco" became a sensation, other chefs are clamoring to get it on their menus as well.

Those chefs learn about the Manglitsa just like the rest of us; YouTube is packed with videos on every imaginable aspect of the pigs. Well known chefs from Europe and the US blog about their passion and exchange tips on how to unlock its seemingly limitless potential.

In person events like PigstockTC, held every October in Traverse City (Michigan's foodie capital), teach American chefs European-style seam butchery and charcuterie, all with a focus on the Mangalitsa pig. (see Pure Mangalitsa video link: http://www.youtube.com/watch?v=Cu-Yj6ZQZy4)

Distinguished presenters include Chef Brian Polcyn, owner of the Forest Grill Restaurant in Birmingham, Michigan, and co-author with Michael Ruhlman of "Charcuterie: The Craft of Salting, Smoking and Curing," as well as Christoph Wiesner, the President of the Austrian Mangalitsa Breeders Association. Up and coming chefs from all over the Midwest come to Traverse City every year to train in the art of the Mangalitsa, just like their East Coast counterparts, who attend a similar event at Mosefund Farms in New Jersey.

Who could have predicted the resurgence of lard with American foodies and fine restaurants? Or that you'd be able to buy Mangalitsa Lard from sites like "chefshop.com" (4 pounds for $50)?

But once The French Laundry, as well as others, like Keith Luce of the highly-praised Herbfarm started using this full-flavored lard, other chefs realized that their light and flaky pie crusts contained a secret weapon; that miraculous lard.

All of this comes on the heels of new research showing that pork fat, or lard, has only half the saturated fat of palm oil, one of American junk food's MVPs. 45% of pork fat is monounsaturated, which can help people raise their good cholesterol and lower the bad. Jennifer McLagan's Award-winning cookbook "Fat: An Appreciation of a Misunderstood Ingredient," says "pork fat is not only useful, but it is also good for us."

Hopefully these pioneers will sway more Americans to return to a more European diet, which includes more animal fats. Most Americans followed this diet until the 1940s, when some potentially-flawed studies linked heart disease to animal fats.

But fortunately, **I believe animal fat's bad reputation is over – consumers should no longer be afraid of them.**

In January, 2009 my friend and long time business partner, Marc Santucci, started raising Mangalitsa feeder pigs in Michigan. When Marc suggested for me to join this business and import breeding stock from Europe, I was thrilled; I've loved Hungary ever since my first visit in 1978. These pigs were an ideal opportunity to build on my previous success in the food business, where I've been active since the 70s.

With American demand consistently exceeding supply, the Mangalitsa is poised to become as popular in America as it is in Europe or Japan.

The curly-haired Mangalitsa is now hailed by many American chefs as the ultimate experience in pork. While traditional pigs like the Berkshire produce an inch of back fat, the Mangalitsa produces between 3 and 4 inches. The Mangalitsa's lighter, airier fat structure allows for whipping of the rendered lard like cream, allowing its use in a variety of dishes unrivalled by any other pork. Or take a look at a Mangalitsa ham, raised in Hungary and cured in Spain. It is one of the world's unforgettable food experiences.

I could go on all day – ask my wife – so I will sign off here and let the 23 Hungarian Chefs in this book take over. They definitely know their Mangalitsas better than just about anyone I've ever met.

I hope this book will open you to some of the Mangalitsa's endless possibilities – and that some of you will share your experiences with us, once you and your families have enjoyed some of these great meals.

Bon Appetit,

Wilhelm W. Kohl

1. NPR, Adee Brown, August 3, 2013
2. NPR Books, Madeleine Brand, June 5, 2006

THE HISTORY OF THE MANGALITSA

WRITTEN BY : PÉTER TÓTH

PRESIDENT OF THE HUNGARIAN NATIONAL ASSOCIATION OF MANGALITSA BREEDERS

It was exactly twenty year's ago that I first tasted Mangalitsa ham. This was one of the reasons why I delightedly accepted the invitation by Péter Széplaki, a book publisher (manager of Boook Publishing House) to contribute in the compilation of a Mangalitsa cookbook and writing its introduction. I will do my best to introduce our beloved breed to you in a simple and interesting way.

The modern history of the Mangalitsa breed began in the hot summer of 1991 by a failing pig farm in Hajdúböszörmény. I was standing by the side of the road with a Spanish friend, who was a prospective vet, wondering what to do... After a six-month long research we found 50 Magalicas which represented a quarter of the entire Magalica stock. We had just been told that these animals were about to be slaughtered, and the two other Mangalitsa gene banks had already decided the liquidation as well, so it was clear that in order to save the breed we had to buy them. They were considered to be fat and slow growing and therefore not profitable in the infiltrating western world. We thought a lot about it, how it would change our lives. What if we don't go back to our academic nightlife? If we proceed to something which may fill up our lives but of which we might not live

to see the outcome? If I said that adventure, challenge, discovering weren't magnetizing us, it would be a lie. To save a breed from dying out would be incredible – after all, how many people can say they've done that?

The decision wasn't easy however. The reputation of the Mangalitsa in the past was highlighted in a few old books as an animal which produced the world's best hams and bacon. Modern opinion is that it is an obsolete breed and not worth keeping. We had more faith in the older accounts of the Mangalitsa and knew, let's say we felt that we'd found what we had been looking for, the world's best raw material for salamis and sausages!

We were watching the last Mangalitsa sows, oblivious to their fate, rumaging around and lying in the mud, happy as the day is long! As were checking out their furry, thick, cylindrical, short body, their leg covered by a rolling, slack skirt of bacon and as they looked at us with a wink under their hairy ear – we simply just fell in love with them. We knew that they didn't give much meat but that mottled meat it did give was full of taste and flavor and delicious - exactly we were looking for. That was the moment I made sense of the saying: "I love you so that I eat you"…

Although the breed was dying out, we had to make the difficult decision of killing one to taste it and another to produce other products like salamis and hams. That reduced the number of Mangalitsas to 198.

That was 21 year's ago. Today, my Spanish friend is one of the world's most famous ham producers and I am President of the Hungarian National Association of Mangalitsa Breeders. The original 200 Mangalitsa has now become 10,000 and our love and passion for the work and for this animal hasn't changed.

THE ACCLIMATIZATION OF MANGALITSA IN HUNGARY

Pigs have always been a very important domestic animal in the Pannonian Basin. The Romans, who originally inhabited the area, were noted for their feasting but also for looking after their animals with great care. They reared the pig known as Szalonta (Napoletanian pig) which was fed with bean and fig, mixed with honey. The animals were eventually killed and filled with quails and roasted in the oven. They were known as Trojan Roasted Pig!

When Hungarians took over pig farming from the Avars the pig was less popular and became a half wild animal living in forests while the diet of the people relied more on fish and poultry. When Hungary Hungary became part of the Ottoman Empire, pork came back into fashion. The Ottoman's religion prohibited pork consumtion, so the invaders didn't take it from the natives. Moreover, the pigs lived well with the native Hungarians at the reedy, tussocky places where they were hiding. So we can say without overstating that the survival of the Hungarians at that time highly depended on pigs. As a result of this close connection, Hungarians not only have funerals for their loved ones, they also have a slaughter ceremony to respect the animal which gives them nourishment throughout the year. While pork was still a key to survival in 16th-17th century Hungary, on the more prosperous European lands gastronomy was doing incredibly well. Guests in the courts of lords and barons were feasting and meateating was the symbol of wealth. Béla Emesei Dorner wrote the following in 1925: 'On the grounds of a guest's notes here is the list of the meats used at a wedding of a German nobleman Wilhelm von Rosenberg in 1578: 370 oxes, 19 wild boar roasts, 2687 wethers, 162 roe deers, 1579 calves, 2292 rabbits, 421 sheep, 470 pheasant, 99 young pig, 276 moor-cocks, 300 porkers, 3910 partridges, 577 porklings, 22687 fieldfares, 88 Westfalian hams, 3000 fat capons, 113 red deers, 12887 hens, 2500 chickens, 24 red deer waist roasts, 98 wild boars, 3550 fat geese.' These unbelievable quantities are due to the fact that the wedding lasted more weeks and besides the hundreds of guests, all dependants were invited to the feast.

In Hungary, no nobleman could afford this laviousness, as, following the Ottoman conquest it developed less quickly than the German trading towns. Ironically, the boost in pork consumption in the 18-19th century is connected to Turkey as well. Turkish wheat (which we now call field corn) wasn't suitable for human consumption but the Hungarians grew it and fed it to their pigs. They eventually started to encourage the pigs to leave the forests and move nearer to their homes, where afterwards they were kept and fed in pens. The first fat, curly-haired pigs came from Serbia to the Ottoman Hungary under the name of „Turkish Pig", 'kondor pigs' and later 'mongulitza'.

In 1833, at the height of the Rascian (Serbian) pig trading, Archduke Joseph Palatine of Hungary visited the estate of Milos, Serbian suzerain in Topčider where he got 9 Sumadia sows and 2 boars as a present. These pigs were kept in Kisjenő (Chișineu-Criș today, Romania, near Arad), and they were cross bred with Romanian pigs from Szalonta and Bakony which was so successful that by the 1850s every affulent Hungarian manor had this breed of pig among its stock. This hugely fat, well growing breed, the Mangalitsa, which provides so much meat was now spreading also to small farms. Besides the original Blonde Mangalitsa new colors became popular, Black, Swallow-bellied, Red and the original Blonde Mangalitsa. And these continue to be developed!

THE TYPES OF MANGALITSA

The most eye-catching feature of the Blonde Mangalitsa is that its body is covered rough, flake-like blonde hair. That furcoat is thin at summer and thick, rough and curly in winter. Blonde Mangalitsa is a typical lard-type hog: its head is quite long, its ears are moderately large, covered with hair curls and leaned forward. The head profile is straight or recede, with a visible jowl, the neck is short and the back cambers slightly upwards. The neck is short and cambered toward the back. The trunk is stocky, but ribs are apparent. The number of paps is about 10 or 12. The bones are elegant, the feet's ends are thin. Its skin is grey, but that color is visible only on the surface and easy to remove together with the outer skin at slaughtering. Its bony, muscular nose (aka digging rim), the eye-lids, eye-lashes, eyebrow, paps and nails are black or slate-grey.

Mangalitsa is not a prolific animal, a sow farrows only 4-8 little striped piglets at once. They grow slowly, their weight is about only 15-17 lbs in the 7-8th weeks. Stripes disappear when piglets are 2 months old. A Blonde porker is the fattest hog in the world. A specimen of 300-320 lbs gives almost 2400 oz rendered lard

besides bacon and flesh. At the Budapest Lard-Type Fair in 1924 there were flocks the members of which gave 73.3% fat of their weight. The majority of the Mangalitsa stock has always been the Blonde, today 75% of the total stock in Hungary is Blonde, which is in fact the original Mangalitsa from Kisjenő. Their number touched bottom in 1993 – only 138 sows existed that time in the whole world – now they are more than 5000, and the number is still increasing.

Black Mangalitsa could be found in other parts of Hungary, mostly in Transdanubia. It grew slower but became bigger than its Blonde colleague and was more resistant against diseases. Unfortunately we have to speak about it in past tense: Black Mangalitsa has gone extinct in the 1970's. Last specimens were seen in the islands of Danube in Serbia.

The Swallow-bellied Mangalitsa breed was produced by crossing the Blonde Mangalitsa and the Black. Its back is black but its belly and the tights' inner sides are blonde. Its qualities are the same as Blonde's, maybe the Swallow-bellied Mangalitsa is a bit more resistant. By 1993 that breed has almost gone extinct too, only 32 sows were known in Hungary. Nowadays we know some hundreds, and fortunately their number started increasing quickly. Red Mangalitsa is a quite new breed, produced by cross-

ing the Blonde Mangalitsa with the Szalonta breed in the 1910's. It was often called an 'Amended Szalonta Mangalitsa' in the old literature but it turned to real Mangalitsa in the 1960's, only its color remained red. By 1993 there was hardly any living specimen of it, only 31 sows were registered. Fortunately this number is slowly increasing, there are 1500 sows today in Hungary.

THE HISTORY OF THE MANGALITSA IN HUNGARY

Mangalitsa was already a popular breed in Hungary in the middle of the 1800s, and some decades later its popularity reached the same peak abroad as well. The golden age lasted about a century. The key of its success was its land-sticking, and so the native Hungarian Mangalitsas can't produce the same quality without the special climate, water, weather and feed of the Carpathian Basin. In the 1840s some Mangalitsas were transported to Silesia hogs degenerated within a few generations. The same phenomenon can be observed nowdays at foreinger Mangalitsa breeders. That land-sticking can be visible even inside Hungary. Once Archduke Joseph Palatine of Hungary personally brought a stock from Kisjenő to Alcsút (the second Mangalitsa stock in the world).

Those hogs looked totally different some years later. The industrialisation and Hungary's latching on to the international trading played a very important role in the Mangalitsa's spreading. It was crucial to found pork fattening farms in order to satisfy big cities' (Vienna, Budapest, Győr, Debrecen) meat demand. The first of them was in Győr in 1840. Hogs were transported here from South by ships and they were forwarded by train to Vienna. The farm had been perished in 1848 but it was rebuilt a few years later with tthe most modern technologies. It was adapted to keep 43.000 Mangalitsas in 50 acres. Just to compare: Mangalitsa breeders in Hungary produced the same quantity in 2012. The capital of Hungary, Budapest *(separately known as Pest, Buda and Old Buda until 1873 – editor's remark)* was also rapidly growing in the 1800s. Urban Mangalitsa feeding were quite chaotic. Hogs were sold not only in streets and at weekly fairs but tricky breeders established plank houses in order to make catering easier – but the smell of hogs destroyed the capital.

Little wonder that local government banned pig farming inside the city in 1847 and new territories were appointed to re-build pig farms in Kőbánya, which was far from the city center that time. Breeders were flexible and they established a huge farm with joint ownership. They bought Mangalitsas from Romania and Serbia at the beginning, l later the animals mostly originated from Hungary. The building of Fatting Farms of Kőbánya was finished in 1870, it was the most modern and biggest pig farm in the world with its 124 acres area and 200.000-hog capacity. These are enormous numbers even today. A new tram-line was built for people to get there and for pigs' transport railway was used. Hungarian Railway Company built three new stations to the area, these still exist and are in use. Fatting Farm of Kőbánya was the central station, industrial railways started there and went to the buildings, transporting feed, animals and excrements. The drainage system and piped water supply were fully built on the farm. Feed-mixing factories, mills, slaughterhouses, salami ripeners, leather factories, soap makers were moved to the other side of the railway. What is more, the fatting farm had its own hotels in order to fix foreigner traders up. 12 governmental vet were working there and

pigs from Kőbánya had great success even in Italy and Switzerland. The average production was 600.000 hogs a year by 1890, but there was a time when 1.000.000 pigs were sold in a year, 35% of which went to Germany. After the success story of Kőbánya, a lot of pig fatting farms were built soon near to Debrecen, Szeged, Pécs, Sopron, Szombathely, Baja, Zombor, Szabadka and Cegléd, among which the farm near Debrecen was the biggest with the capacity of 100 000 animals..

Besides huge farms, rural Mangalitsa breeding was flourishing as well in the 19th century. Almost every countryside household had Mangalitsas, it gave the food for the family in a whole year. All facts above show that Mangalitsa's spreading was not a central decision but a proper answer to the market's demand. The upswing of the Mangalitsa breeding had a great impact on Hungarian cuisine too, lard became popular, frying in deep fat with red paprika powder became major cooking method. Salami-producing also started spreading at this time, mostly coming from Slovakian and kraut minority. Kraut meat products and Csabai sausage with its Slovakian origin are trademarks even today.

At the beginning of the 20th century quick growing, more reproductive meat hog types, such as Yorkshire or Flat pig appeared in Hungary, too. Since they give cheaper meat in shorter time, the Mangalitsa started decreasing. Cooking oil, electricity and refrigerators were the mort on the breed in the 1950s. It was no longer a problem to keep meat fresh for long time – lard's price went down, meat's price rocketed up. The

taste and quality weren't relevant, the only important aspect was to produce huge amount of meat as cheap as possible. Government-controlled pig breeding cared about Mangalitsa no longer, it was too complicated, by 1960 it got out of the eyesight of the public awareness, and almost became extinct by the 1970s. Gene banks were founded only in 1974 where the last few hundred sows were vegetating until the regime change. Finally the gene bank system collapsed too, sows were trasported to slaughterhouses and the breed was about to disappear from the Earth.

A newly emerged market demand arrived at the ultimate moment. Living Mangalitsas have been registered, Hungarian National Association of Mangalitsa Breeders was founded and a new marketing and producing system was started which is able to maintain subsistence of the breed for a long time. Today there are 10.000 controlled sows and the same quantity of Mangalitsa in small farms. It seems, the danger of extinction is over!

THE PRESENT AND FUTURE OF THE MANGALITSA

It was necessary to work out a new approach in gene-saving, gene-keeping, producing and marketing in order to make Mangalitsa, as a premium product popular again. Poor people's cheap meat turned to be a rare, expensive delicacy. We shall keep our values from the past, but we have to keep only things which are worth keeping. Mangalitsa is more than a hog.

Integrating old things into new relations always gener-

15. ábra. Magyar mangalicza sertések.

ates resistance. Many people think that everything was better in the past and they want to have back that past with no changes. But that doesn't work. Everything changes. Hereby a citation by Károly Monostori, a professor of the Hungarian Royal Veterinary Academy, from his book 'The basics of pig farming' in 1897: 'I don't state that tricks and traditions in pig farming that came from our fathers are unprofitables, but I do state that new times gave new utensils and methods, and using them is in our interest.' Mangalitsa shows a new point of view: it has old-fashioned values it changes in order to maintain the breed and to give the opportunity of knowing Mangalitsa for generations. The most important change is that quality dominates when it comes to breeding Mangalitsa and producing food in the end. There might be cheaper meat, but there is no better one.

Mangalitsa had almost gone extinct because it hadn't been changed during 160 years, a sow today looks the same as it did in 1833. It is the only pig which has always given a standard quality. It is an old breed but also meets every requirement of our time.

Mangalitsa is more than an animal, it is a symbol. The last herald of the golden age of Hungarian agriculture which gives us hope to reach that peak again. It gives the best meat in the world and the best dishes and sausages are made of it. But it needs professionals. Mangalitsa can be successful only in the hands of aducated meat traders, cooks and chefs. This book offers the opportunity to Hungary's best cooks and chefs to tell their experiences and to show us how to put the world's best pork meat on the table.

Therefore Mangalitsa is not only a symbol, it is our common denominator. That connects us finally, as Hungarian ingredients transform into culinary experiences. Mangalitsa could make Hungary world-known. There are loads of reasons to be proud of it, irrespectively of sex, age or politics. There is no better feeling than eating well together, it has been a symbol of peace and good relation since the ancient times. May it be today, too!

ENJOY YOUR READING AND MEAL!
The text is edited by Jason B. Kohl

The Hungarian - Netherlands - USA
MANGALITSA CONNECTION
Written by : Wilhelm W. Kohl

It was Austrian exporters who first introduced the Mangalitsa pig to countries outside the former Austro-Hungarian Empire, including the U.K. & the U.S. about 10 years ago. Although original populations of pigs exist in basically all the Panonian Basin countries, including remnant populations of the famous "Black Mangalitsa" in Serbia, effective breeding of the species has only been done in Hungary for the last 2 decades.

It was impossible to legally acquire Mangalitsa breeding stock from Hungary until 2014, when we finally reached an agreement between Pure Mangalitsa LLC & MOE, the Hungarian National Association of Mangalitsa Breeders, to that effect. But importing live pigs directly from Hungary to the U.S. is still impossible due to the lack of a formal protocol between the USDA and the Hungarian Health Authorities.

Fortunately, Hungary is now part of the European Union (E.U.) and many Western European countries do have established protocols.

On the picture: Barbara Meyer zu Altenschildesche – breeder, Willhelm W. Kohl – owner of Pure Mangalitsa, Péter Tóth –President of the Hungarian National Association of Mangalitsa Breeders

ALL ABOUT BARBARA

Thanks to social media, and Facebook in particular, I got to meet Barbara.

Barbara Meyer zu Altenschildesche is absolutely unique and amazing when it comes to working with the "Royal Mangalitsas", as she likes to call them. Born to landed gentry in Germany and trained as a graphic designer in Cologne, she was given an abandoned wild piglet in April 2009. Her son Niels had found it in the garden of their country home in Leuvenum, a beautiful rural area of Holland. She immediately fell in love with the piglet and decided to raise it by hand. Eventually the little piglet, named Anne, became a completely tame wild pig, and Barbara decided to look for some companions for Anne. While a completely tame wild pig is quite rare in itself, and despite Barbara's complete lack of farming experience, she was able to locate some pure-breed red Mangalitsa pigs in Austria, which she imported and raised on a small parcel of open land near her home in 2011.

But once the red haired Mangalitsas arrived, they became Barbara's passion.

Her boar, who she named Igor, and her two sows, Yana and Ilona, quickly produced many beautiful red piglets. Their happy Manga-family quickly became the best-cared-for and most-photographed pigs in the world.

Barbara, also a dedicated student of German mythology, was of course quite familiar with the mystical Freya, the German goddess of fertility, frequently depicted with her constant companion Hildisvini, a Golden Boar. So Igor quickly became Barbara's Hildisvini, just like in the ancient saga. He and the others in her care are some of luckiest pigs alive.

Barbara cares for her animals like nobody else in the pig business; not only has she raised all her piglets to be hand tame, she spends endless hours every day learning every detail of their behavior in free-range conditions.

Barbara loves to model for pictures with her "Royal Reds," sometimes in costume. These photos show nature in unparalleled harmony between humans and animals. She is also at the forefront of promoting socially responsible animal husbandry. Reintroducing species-appropriate production of the world's most popular food animal to a wider consumer audience has become one of Barbara's major goals in life.

Promoting the Mangalitsa pigs themselves, for certain some of the best tasting pork in the world, certainly goes along with that goal. And after meeting Barbara in person on a trip to Austria and Hungary in January 2014, I did not have to ask her twice about cooperating with us to establish a truly diversified and sustainable population in North America.

For more details you can read all about the events that followed on her "Mangalitza Breed" Facebook page or on her blog https://mangalitzablog.wordpress.com.

Enjoy the pictures and enjoy the great dishes that this Trans-European connection was able to provide.

THE MEAT
OF MANGALITSA

FABRICATED HAM
FOR PROSCIUTTO

BELLY FABRICATED FOR
PANCETTA OR BACON

WHOLE HAM
UN-FABRICATED

BACK FAT FOR LARDO

TENDERLOIN

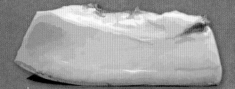

CHEEK

SHOULDER

PICNIC

Lo

R

BI

LOIN WITH
FAT CAP INTACT

COLLAR MUSCLE

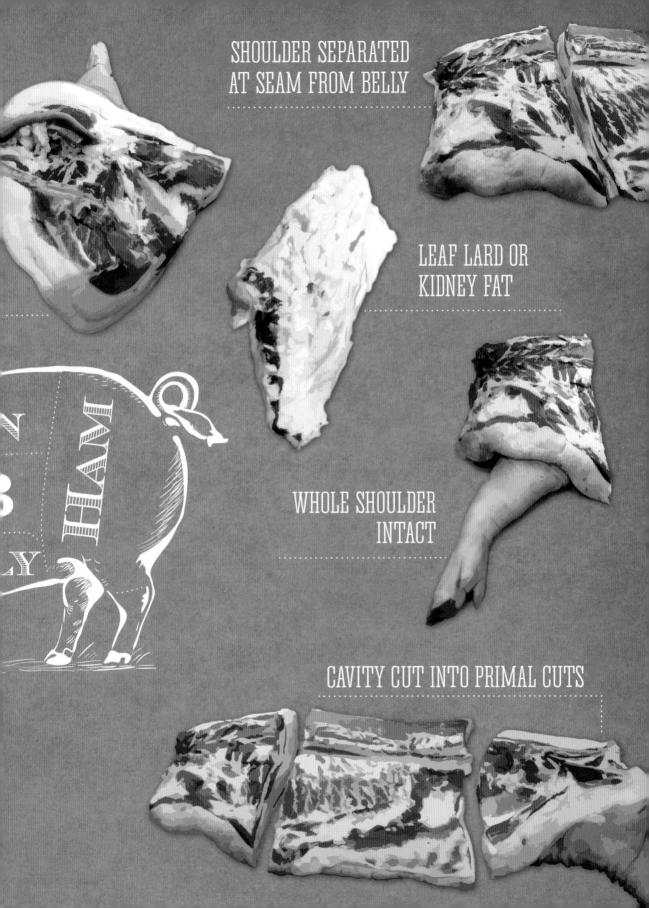

SHOULDER SEPARATED
AT SEAM FROM BELLY

LEAF LARD OR
KIDNEY FAT

WHOLE SHOULDER
INTACT

CAVITY CUT INTO PRIMAL CUTS

RECEPIES

FERENC BALÁZS
ANDRÁSSY RESIDENCY

Ferenc Balázs takes his inspiration from combinations of tastes, colors and techniques and enjoys experimenting from talented young colleagues. He enjoys to experiment, offering vanilla with carrot and red cabbage purée with cinnamon as a garnish for pork confit. He soars when there are no compromises and when his guests are satisfied after having eaten a dish dreamed and made by him – and he's got great opportunities for this as the chef of the Accent Hotel Management.

'Although Hungarian cuisine is not yet unique and is in its infancy, it is constantly developing. We try to change Hungarian cuisine to fit into European traditions. Many Hungarian chefs feel that the biggest problem is the lack of ingredients and suppliers but, as I see, that is improving, too. I source many products, like cheese and organic vegetables from small local farmers, and I am confident that these products stand their ground even in the finest kitchens. Fish and seafood, sourced locally are my strongest inspirations, but since I've been working here local ingredientes inspire me the most. We buy Mangalitsa meat from local breeders. I love using it for roasting or as a steak but I often use it to make salamis or aged hams, too, because it is juicier, softer and tastier than other pork.'

MANGALITSA BRAIN IN PIEROGI

INGREDIENTS (FOR 4 PERSONS):

FOR THE FILLING:
10.5 oz / 300 g Mangalitsa brain
2 tsps / 10 g salvia
1 onion, finely chopped
1 egg
1 tbsp Parmesan cheese, grated
salt, ground white pepper to taste
olive oil

FOR THE PASTA:
4 cups / 500 g white pierogi
10 egg yolks
+ 2 egg yolks for glazing
8 boiled egg yolks, grated
pinch of salt

FOR THE GRAVY:
2 egg yolks
1/2 cup / 0.1 l heavy cream
1/4 cup / 50 g butter
1 lemon

FOR THE ASPARAGUS:
14 oz / 400 g green asparagus
1/2 lemon juice
7 oz / 200 g onion, finely chopped
1/2 cup / 100 g butter
salt, freshly ground black pepper to taste

RECOMMENDED WINE
PATRICIUS WINE HOUSE
Tokaji Furmint, 2011

Trim membranes from brain and rinse in cold water. Sauté onion on olive oil then add salvia, eggs, Parmesan cheese and brain. Season with salt and pepper and sear to doneness.

Combine all ingredients of the pasta, wrap in foil and put in the refrigerator for 1 hour. Roll out pasta to thin and cut rounds by a wavy edge cutter (diameter: cca. 3 inch). Glaze the edges with beated egg yolks. Spoon filling in the center of the rounds and cover with an other pasta round. Cook in salty boiling water.

Pour cream in a saucepan, add egg yolks and, over lightly boiling water, beat it until thick. Melt butter in a pot then remove from heat and add to gravy. Flavor with lemon juice and salt.

Blanch the cleaned asparagus then refresh in order to preserve its color and crispness. Sauté onion on butter then add asparagus. Season with salt and pepper then blend with cooked pasta. Serving: Put pasta rounds on the plate with asparagus ragout then pour gravy by them.

'PIG DUET' WITH VANILLA-CARROT AND FRAGRANT CABBAGE

INGREDIENTS (FOR 4 PERSONS):

FOR THE 'PIG DUET':
21 oz / 600 g Mangalitsa chop
(untrimmed, with skin)
21 oz / 600 g Mangalitsa shoulder
36 oz / 1 kg Mangalitsa lard
3.5 oz / 100 g carrot, sliced
3.5 oz / 100 g parsley root, sliced
2 sprigs rosemary
1/2 cup / 0.1 l white wine
2 tbsps / 50 g salt

FOR THE VANILLA-CARROT:
10.5 oz / 300 g carrot, diced
3/4 cup / 200 g butter
1 Vanilla bean

FOR THE FRAGRANT CABBAGE:
10.5 oz red cabbage, grated | 30 dkg
2 star anises
1 cinnamon stick
1/4 cup sugar | 5 dkg
1 tbsp wine vinegar | 2 cl

Preheat oven to 150°F (65°C). Wash and trim fat from chop, sprinkle with salt and pepper. Trim shoulder, cut off and mince the bigger part of it (0.2-inch meat should rest on the skin). Sprinkle minced meat with salt and pepper. Fill it into shoulder skin and roll up tight. Render lard, add vegetables and rosemary then put meat in it. Confit in oven for 12 hours. Remove meat from lard. Add wine to gravy, bring to a boil then drain. Thicken with butter before serving.

Steam carrot dices on a small amount of butter with Vanilla bean.

Caramelize sugar then add grated cabbage. Season with salt, cinnamon and star anise. Steam covered until tender. Add some wine vinegar, purée in a blender and push through a sieve.

Serving: Heat oven to 430°F (220°C). Bake meat slices until crispy and golden brown. Serve with garnishes on a plate.

RECOMMENDED WINE
PATRICIUS WINE HOUSE
Tokaji Katinka, 2008

NUT PIE WITH LEMON SORBET

INGREDIENTS (FOR 4 PERSONS):

FOR THE PIE:
1 1/4 / 150 g cups flour
3 eggs
2/3 cup / 150 g butter
2.5 oz / 70 g walnut, ground
1/2 cup / 100 g sugar
1 tsp baking powder
1/4 cup / 50 g sour cream

FOR THE WHITE CHOCOLATE TOPPING:
1.6 oz / 40 g white chocolate
1.7 oz / 50 g mascarpone
2 egg yolks
1/2 cup / 50 ml heavy cream
1 tbsp / 10 g vanilla sugar
2 tbsps / 20 g gelatin
2 limes
5.5 oz / 150 g whipped cream
5.5 oz / 150 g blackberry

FOR THE SORBET:
7 oz / 200 g lemon
7 tbsps / 100 g syrup
7 oz / 200 g apple, grated
2 egg whites

FOR THE ORANGE CRISP:
1/2 cup / 100 g butter
1/2 cup / 70 g flour
1 cup / 100 g icing sugar
1/4 cup / 50 ml orange juice

Preheat oven to 355°F (180°C) . Cream butter with eggs, sour cream and sugar then add sieved flour, walnut and baking powder. Spoon pastry in a lightly oiled and floured muffin tins. Bake for about 10 minutes without air circulation.

Melt white chocolate over a pot of lightly boiling water then add cream and stir slowly. Beat egg yolks with mascarpone then add it to the cream-chocholate mixture. Add Vanilla sugar and flesh of limes then blend gently with whipped cream and melted gelatin.

Mix lemon juice with syrup and grated apple then add the whipped egg whites. Put it into the deep-freeze and beat it with a whisk in every 15 minutes until we can form it with a spoon. May be prepared in ice cream maker as well.

Heat oven to 250°F (120°C). Combine all ingredients and transfer pastry to a parchment-lined baking sheet. Pastry shall be very thin. Bake and dry in oven until crispy.

Serving: Cut off the top of pies and put one spoon of chocolate cream on it. Place a blackberry on the top. Cover with a layer of cream on demand. Serve with sorbet and orange crisp.

RECOMMENDED WINE
PATRICIUS WINE HOUSE
Tokaji Aszú, 2006

TAMÁS BEREZNAY

Tamás Bereznay, who used to cook regularly to the President of Hungary has known since he can remember that he would be a cook. Now he regurarly cooks on television and writes cookery books. His greatest motivation is delighting his guests and offering them something they haven't seen or tasted before and then seeing the joy on their faces when they've discovered something new. What he loves most is to discover new things and meals by preparing an everyday commodity with different ingredients, spices or heat treatment.

'I love Hungarian cuisine because it is extremely diverse. We have a wide variety of vegetables throughout the country, from Borsod to Pécs, Sopron to Szeged, and I haven't mentioned the meat yet! We have lamb, goat, cattle, river fish from bighead carp to carassius – or game, from pheasant to deer. Hungarian meat cuisine is extremely varied but the well-kept Mangalitsa stands out as one of the best ever as being more juicy and tasty than other meats and is so versatile. The latter is very important to me because my strongest inspiration is how I can make meals with different tastes, consistencies or types of one commodity. That's why spices are my favourite commodities. Parsley and garlic most of all (together and separately), but I use a lot of cumin, ginger, chili, coriander and caraway-seed. Amongst my colleagues It may not be surprising that amongst my colleagues I also follow... the works of the ones in whom I find the same temperament and spiciness. Among my fellow chefs, I regard Marco Pierre White and Giorgio Locatelli as my teachers.'

SIDE BACON BAKED IN BEER

INGREDIENTS (FOR 4 PERSONS):

53 oz / 1.5 kg side bacon, thin
4 cloves of garlic, finely chopped
4 sprigs thyme
1 tsp sea salt
1 lemon, zest
4 cups / 1 l wheat beer
1/4 cup / 50 ml olive oil

Blend thyme leaves, garlic, lemon zest, salt and olive oil. Brush fleshy side of bacon with the mixture and roll up tight. Truss if necessary. Place into a baking bag, pour beer and lemon juice on. Close tight or squeeze air out from bag and put in the refrigerator for 24 hours.

Preheat oven to 285°F (140°C) the follow-up day. Transfer bacon in a baking pan, brush with marinade and bake it for 3.5 hours without air circulation. Baste regurarly. Pack in foil when done and set aside. Serve in thin slices and garnish with fresh lettuce salad and homemade sour cherry jam.

RECOMMENDED BEER
LINDEMANS KRIEK

MANGALITSA CHUCK WITH BAKED BEANS AND TOMATOES

INGREDIENTS (FOR 4 PERSONS):

28 oz / 800 g Mangalitsa spare rib
21 oz / 600 g wax bean
8 tomatoes, medium
2/3 cup / 0.15 l olive oil
Maldon salt
salt, freshly ground black pepper

RECOMMENDED WINE
VÁLIBOR
Siller, 2011

Cut meat lengthwise into two pieces and place them into 3% brine for 2 hours. Remove from brine, pat dry, spread with ground pepper and put into a vacuum-sealed bag. Brush with olive oil, seal and bake in oven for 16 hours (with air circulation) at 160°F (70°C).

Preheat oven to 375°F (190°C). Wash beans, break off the ends and transfer them onto a parchment-lined baking sheet. Sprinkle with olive oil, Maldon salt and freshly ground pepper. Bake for 15-20 minutes without air circulation.

Boil a pot of water. Cut an X on the bottom of tomatoes. Submerge them in the boiling water for 30 seconds then remove with a slotted spoon and peel away the skin. Sauté peeled tomatoes on olive oil. Serving: Cut chuck into thick slices and sear them on all sides in olive oil. Garnish with baked beans and tomato.

CHOCOLATE ICE CREAM WITH MANGALITSA CRACKLINGS AND CHILI

INGREDIENTS (FOR 4 PERSONS):

5.5 oz / 150 g Valrhona Guanaja
80% dark chocolate
1/3 cup / 75 g brown muscovado sugar
1/3 cup / 75 g cane sugar
1 tbsp cocoa powder
4 egg yolks
2 cups / 0.5 l heavy cream
1.8 oz / 50 g Mangalitsa crackling,
finely chopped
2 chili peppers
2 tsps Maldon salt

Melt chocolate over a pot of lightly boiling water. Cream egg yolks with sugar, add cocoa powder stirring constantly.

Boil cream and combine with the mixture. Stir it slowly and add melted chocolate to it spoon by spoon. Stir well, cool and transfer it to an ice cream maker. (If you don't have an ice cream maker, pour mixture to a thick metal bowl which you have already chilled in the freezer. Put it into the deep-freeze and frost it. Beat with a whisk in every 30 minutes.) Add the cracklings, chili and salt before it frosts totally.

RECOMMENDED WINE
TAMÁS WINE CELLAR
Syrah, 2009

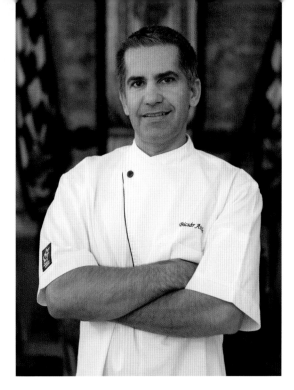

ATTILA BICSÁR

ALABÁRDOS

Attila Bicsár, one of the leading personalities of Hungarian gastronomy feels that the most important thing about food is taste built on provincial flavors. He works in a restaurant located in Buda Castle where most of the diners are tourists from abroad or other parts of Hungary. This prize-winning chef enjoys using local ingredients in a bold and innovative way to surprise his guests by cooking individually for them.

'I find it important that guests understand that they eat a really tasty, modern-looking dish which is not over-complicated. Hungarian ingredients offer a challenge for reform but it is that challenge that makes Hungarian cuisine more modern and exciting. I'm inspired by my beloved wife and two daughters when cooking 'everyday' dishes at home for them. Parsley, dill, squash, ewe cheese, poppy seed, apricot, egg barley, red paprika powder, duck liver, goose liver, crackling - so many favorites! Using these ingredients should make Hungarian cuisine successful abroad. The great example of this is the Mangalitsa pig. The breeding is so well controlled, I hope that chefs will experiment with it when they realise that it is a superior product and will become a big hit abroad and in Hungarian restaurants as well'

CAESAR SALAD HUNGARIAN STYLE

INGREDIENTS (FOR 4 PERSONS):
1 Romaine lettuce
4 thin slices of Mangalitsa ham
4 thin slices of Mangalitsa bacon

FOR THE DRESSING:
2 egg yolks
2/3 cup / 0.2 l grape seed oil
cca. 2 oz / 60 g Mangalitsa sausage, thin sliced
1 tbsp Dijon mustard
1 clove of garlic, grated
1/2 cup / 0.1 l sour cream
salt, freshly ground black pepper

FOR THE PASTA STICKS:
2 cups / 250 g flour
0.2 oz / 6 g yeast
1/4 cup / 50 g olive oil
1/2 cup / 50 g icing sugar
1 tbsp / 20 ml white wine
1/2 cup / 0.1 l water
4.5 oz / 125 g Mangalitsa lard
3/4 tsp / 6 g salt
2 cloves of garlic, grated

Put sausage slices in a nonstick pan and fry on their own fat. Remove slices with a slotted spoon and place them on a paper towel. Set aside the rendered fat.

Heat oven to 320°F (160°C). Put bacon slices between two sheets of greaseproof paper, press down and bake for 10 minutes with air circulation.

Preheat oven to 390°F (200°C). Combine all ingredients and form pastry into walnut sized balls. Roll balls into thin sticks. Place them on a baking sheet and bake for 6 minutes with air circulation until crispy and golden brown. When cool enough to handle, roll ham slices over sticks.

Blend egg yolks with Dijon mustard, stirring constantly. Add oil step by step, rendered lard, garlic, sour cream, salt and pepper. Wash lettuce thoroughly and tear into bite sized pieces. Mix lettuce gently with dressing, then toss with sausages and bacons. May be garnished with parsley oil or leaves. Instead of sticks you can serve it with toasted bread cubes and garlic as well.

RECOMMENDED WINE
SAUSKA
Tokaj Cuvée 113, 2009

PRESSED-STUFFED FLANK STEAK WITH LECHO PURÉE, BUTTERNUT SQUASH AND DILL JELLY

INGREDIENTS (FOR 4 PERSONS)
FOR THE FLANK STEAK:
4 bread rolls
1/2 cup / 0.1 l milk
2 hard boiled eggs, grated
1 fresh egg
2 cloves of garlic, grated
1 bunch of parsley, finely chopped
21 oz / 600 g Mangalitsa flank
1/2 cup / 100 g heavy cream
salt, pepper, ground caraway seed to taste

FOR THE BUTTERNUT SQUASH:
21 oz butternut squash, shredded | 60 dkg
1 onion, finely chopped
1 shallot, Julienne cut
2 tomatoes, Julienne cut
1 bell pepper, yellow, Julienne cut
3/4 cup sour cream | 20 dkg
salt to taste, white wine vinegar, sugar, oil

FOR THE LECHO PURÉE
(lecsó, Hungarian style vegetable stew):
1.5 oz / 50 g Mangalitsa bacon, diced
1 tbsp Mangalitsa lard
2 onions, finely chopped
4 cloves of garlic, finely chopped
5 bell peppers, yellow, chopped
2 tomatoes, peeled
1 chili pepper
salt, red paprika powder, ground caraway seed

RECOMMENDED WINE
BUSSAY WINE CELLAR
Csörnyeföldi Szürkebarát (Pinot gris), 2009

Soak bread rolls in milk for 5 minutes. Squeeze milk out then add eggs, garlic and parsley. Blend thoroughly and season with salt and pepper. Cut flank into two pieces horizontally and form it in a rectangular shape. Mince trimmed meat strips and mix with cream, salt, pepper and ground caraway seed. Cut meat into two pieces crosswise, spread with salt and pepper. Preheat oven to 285°F (140°C). Place one piece of flank into a greased flameproof dish. Spoon the half of the meat mixture onto, then spread with the stuffing, then with the other half of the meat mixture. Cover with the other piece of flank. Put one tbsp lard on the top then bake for 2.5 hours without air circulation. Press down when done and cool. Slice and warm in shallow fat before serving.

Sauté onion on oil. Add the 2/3 of butternut squash and salt and steam for 10-15 minutes. Add sour cream, boil and purée in a blender. Flavor with wine vinegar and sugar. Heat oil, add tomatoes, paprika and shallot. Warm up vegetables then add the leftover butternut squash to the mixture and sprinkle with salt.

Render bacon dices and sauté onion and garlic on it until golden brown. Add more lard if needed. Sprinkle with red paprika powder and pour a small amount of water on it. Add pepper, and tomatoes a few minutes later. Season with salt and ground caraway seed, cook for 20 minutes. Purée in a blender and sieve.

Throw a bunch of dill into boiling water, refresh and tap them dry. Purée in a blender with water, add some salt and sieve. Soak gelatin leaves in cold water then add them to the heated dill mixture. Pour it into a shallow dish and put in the refrigerator for 3 hours. Cut rounds from solid jelly. You may put dill into the butternut squash as well.

CURD CHEESE SQUARE RÁKÓCZI STYLE

INGREDIENTS (FOR 4 PERSONS):
FOR THE PASTRY:
1/4 cup / 60 g salted butter
2 tbsps Mangalitsa lard
1/4 cup / 40 g sugar
2 egg yolks
1 cup / 125 g flour
1/2 tbsp baking powder
pinch of salt

FOR THE CURD CHEESE TOPPING:
1 egg
2 egg yolks
1/2 cup / 100 g sugar
1 cup / 250 g curd cheese
2 1/2 gelatin leaves
1/2 lemon, juice and zest
1/2 Vanilla bean
1 3/4 / 400 g cups heavy cream

FOR THE ALMOND PASTRY:
2 layers of strudel pastry
1 tbsp butter
1 tbsp almond, sliced

FOR THE SERVING:
2 egg whites
2 tbsps sugar
2 tbsps basil sugar
8 tbsps homemade apricot jam

RECOMMENDED WINE
PELLE WINE CELLAR
Zsófia Cuvée, 2009

Preheat air circulating oven to 355°F (180°C). Cream lard and butter with sugar. Add egg yolks, one at a time, whipping constantly. Combine sifted flour, salt and baking powder. Mix gently with butter cream and pat pastry into a rectangular baking pan. and bake pastry until golden brown (about 10-12 minutes). Cut into 10 slices when still warm.

Mix eggs and egg yolks with sugar and warm it over a pot of lightly boiling water. Whip until cool. Sieve curd cheese (or smooth it with a blender), then add egg foam, lemon zest, lemon juice and seeds of Vanilla bean. Soak gelatin leaves in cold water until soften. Squeeze and melt the leaves in warm water then add to egg mixture. Whip cream slowly until it becomes gentle foam then add to egg mixture. Pour cream into a pan and put into the refrigerator. Cut into 10 slices when solid.

Preheat the oven to 390°F (200°C). Brush one layer of strudel pastry with melted butter. Spread with icing sugar then cover with the other layer of strudel pastry. Brush it with butter again then spread with icing sugar and almond. Cut pastry into rectangles and place them onto a parchment-lined baking sheet. Bake them until crispy, without air circulation (about 6-8 minutes).

Heat oven to 355°F (180°C). Whip egg whites with a whisk. Add sugar and whip until fluffy. Spoon it into a decorating bag and squeeze mixture over a plate. Dry foam in oven for 5 minutes with air circulation, then go on baking at 250°F (120°C) for 8 minutes, without air circulation.

Serving: Spread pastries with apricot jam, place curd cheese foam on them. Put almond pastry on the top. Decorate the plate with baked foam and jam drops. Dust with icing sugar.

LAJOS BÍRÓ

BOCK BISTRO

Lajos Bíró, leader of Bock Bistros is said to be provocative, outspoken and anarchical. He is a self-proclaimed perfectionist whose philosophy is that it takes equal time to do things badly or well, so chooses to do them well.

'I find that the ancient, traditional Hungarian cuisine was more delicate and consumer-friendly than modern one. Traditional cooking uses lots of spices and unusual ingredients unlike modern dishes which tend to be more uniform. While it's important to remember our traditions, it's also important that we don't stick so rigidly to them, that we don't allow our cuisine to evolve. My goal is to re-create traditional dishes in a modern way. I try to create original dishes using the best of ingredients which means I can't always just use Hungarian ingredients. I'm hugely motivated by the combination of ingredients, flavors and consistencies. Mangalitsa offers all three, being fat and juicy which contributes to its texture and taste. It has a great future, just as the black-legged pig.'

MANGALITSA TARTARE
WITH WASABI-AND-APPLE TART

INGREDIENTS (FOR 4 PERSONS):
FOR THE TARTARE:

18 oz / 500 g Mangalitsa tenderloin
1 tsp salt
freshly ground black pepper
parsley and chive (finely chopped) for decorating

FOR THE VINAIGRETTE-MIX:

2 pickled cucumbers
2 shallots
1 tbsp caper berry
1/2 cup / 0.1 l extra virgin olive oil

FOR THE APPLE TART:

1 tsp wasabi powder
2 tbsps mayonnaise (good quality)
2 Granny Smith apples

Trim membranes from tenderloin, cut into bigger pieces then season with salt and pepper. Grind it and let minced meat fall from meat grinder directly onto the plate, in order to keep its shape and pattern in original form. Sprinkle with parsley and chive.

Dice all ingredients of vinaigrette-mix and blend with oil. Spread the mix on the plate, and put minced meat on it (freshly from the grinder). Do it right before serving!

Cut apples into 1/10-inch slices. Mix wasabi powder with water then add mayonnaise. Layer apple slices and mayonnaise and serve as a side-dish with the tartare.

(Editor's remarks: it is important to prepare this food only from fresh ingredients, meat must be not older than half day!)

RECOMMENDED WINE
BOCK
Rosé, 2013

MANGALITSA CHOP WITH OCTOPUS, BLACK PUDDING AND POTATOES ANNA STYLE

INGREDIENTS (FOR 4 PERSONS):
4 slices (8.8 oz / 250 g of each) Mangalitsa chop
olive oil

FOR THE GRAVY:
1.5 oz / 50 g Mangalitsa ham, finely chopped
1/2 onion, finely chopped
2 button mushrooms, finely chopped
1 sprig thyme
1 tsp tomato purée
1/2 cup / 0.1 l demi glace
1 tbsp balsamic vinegar
1/2 cup / 0.1 l heavy cream
1/2 cup / 0.1 l sour cream

FOR THE OCTOPUS:
1 baby octopus
12 cups / 3 l water
4 bay leaves, whole
1 tsp red paprika powder
1/2 chili, pitted
1 clove of garlic, grated

FOR THE POTATOES:
12 potatoes, medium
1/2 cup / 0.1 l heavy cream
1/2 cup / 100 g butter, melted
7 oz / 200 g black pudding (made with bread roll)

RECOMMENDED WINE
BOCK WINE CELLAR
Cabernet Franc Fekete-hegy Selection,
2011

Preheat oven to 350°F (180°C). Sprinkle chop slices with salt and pepper. Sear slices on shallow fat. Leave slices in the pan and put into oven. Bake for 6-7 minutes and set aside to a lukewarm place for 4-5 minutes.

Sauté minced ham in a pan. Add onion first, stir well then put finely chopped mushroom to pan as well. Add the rest of the ingredients: thyme first, then tomato, demi glace and balsamic vinegar. Heavy cream and sour cream should be the last ones. Fry mixture well. Purée in a blender when done.

Put octopus into a pot of water. Bring to a boil and simmer slowly until tender. Cut off arms. Take out a small amount of cooking water. Blend with bay leaves, red paprika, chili and garlic in order to get a thick pulp. Brush octopus arms with the marinade.

Heat the oven to 325°F (160°C). Peel potatoes and cut into paper-thin slices. Brush a casserole dish with butter. Place a layer of potatoes into the casserole. A slice should cover the half of the previous one. Sprinkle with salt, pepper then brush with butter and cream. Spread a layer of black pudding's filling. Repeat layering process until you come to your final layer, which should be potato. The more layers you have the more spectacular the dish is. Bake it until tender (30-40 minutes). Poke a toothpick into. When it slides in with no resistance you have a done dish. Cool it pressed down. It is recommended to prepare the day before. It is easier to slice and flavors have time to mix together.

Serving: Place some gravy on the plate. Put meat and octopus on the top and garnish with potato.

ICE CREAM WITH BACON AND TOMATO JAM

INGREDIENTS (FOR 4 PERSONS):
FOR THE ICE CREAM:
1 cup / 0.25 l milk
1 cup / 0.25 l heavy cream
cca. 5 egg yolks (3.5 oz / 100 g)
1 Vanilla bean
1/2 cup / 100 g sugar

FOR THE TOMATO JAM:
4 tbsps homemade apricot jam
1 tomato
4 fresh basil leaves

FOR THE SERVING:
6 slices of Mangalitsa bacon

Make a Crème Anglaise first. Warm up milk and cream. Beat egg yolks with sugar. Blend the two mixture thoroughly and add seeds of Vanilla bean. Heat it until thicken. The temperature must not exceed 181°F (83°C) where eggs set. Drain when done and cool, then place in the deep-freeze and frost it. Stir it time to time until reaches the desired consistency (can be prepared in ice cream maker as well).

Boil a pot of water. Cut an X on the bottom of the tomato. Submerge it in boiling water for 30 seconds then remove with a slotted spoon and peel away the skin. Remove seeds. Dice tomato flesh into 0.2-inch cubes and mix into apricot jam with the finely chopped basil.

Fry bacon slices and pat dry. Place bacon on the ice cream, finely chopped or in whole. Pour tomato jam on the top and serve.

RECOMMENDED WINE
BOCK WINE CELLAR
Göntéri Hárslevelű, 2008

LÁSZLÓ BODÓCS

BISTORANT
FOUR POINTS BY SHERATON

Under cover of my work I have travelled a lot in Hungary, from East to West, and wherever I appeared I always wanted to get aquainted with local flavors, foods and commodities. I think for a traveller it has to be very important to be able to distinguish regional foods. I returned to my home county, properly speaking, to Kecskemét, not so long ago and I enjoy this kind of investigation. There are a lot of Mangalica breeders in the Great Hungarian Plain. I was lucky enough to find an organic Mangalitsa farm, that's where I have my excellent meats, sausages, salamis, pâtés in with the generous help of my friend Pál Lakó.

'Our traditions must be kept well with a special focus not only on culture but on our foods and commodities. It is important not to forget these materials, but use them and keep abreast of the times. I offer here mille-feuille with cracklings and plum as a dessert - that is my favorite here. I did my best to keep an eye on the tradition and on the original version - and create a lighter version of different ingredients. That's what I think of Hungarian romance: respect to te past and reform served on the same plate.'

PIG'S HEAD CARPACCIO WITH PUMPKIN PURÉE AND PARSLEY SALAD

INGREDIENTS (FOR 4 PERSONS):
FOR THE CARPACCIO:
18 oz / 500 g Mangalitsa head meat
36 oz / 1 kg Mangalitsa lard
1/4 cup / 70 g salt
2 tbsps / 30 g sugar
18 oz / 500 g mixed vegetables (carrot, celery
root, parsley root, onion, garlic)
fresh spices (rosemary, thyme, bay leaf,
parsley, leek)

FOR THE PARSLEY SALAD:
2 bunches of parsley
2 shallots
1/2 lemon
3 tbsps poppy seed oil
1 tsp Dijon mustard
1 tsp honey
salt, black pepper, ground

FOR THE PUMPKIN PURÉE:
10.5 oz / 300 g pumpkin
1/2 orange
1 tsp ginger, grated
1 tbsp pumpkin seed oil
pinch of cinnamon
1 tsp honey
pinch ot ground nutmeg, salt

FOR THE SERVING:
smoked Mangalitsa tongue
poppy seed oil
pickled green walnuts

Boil 4 cups of water with salt, sugar, 1 bunch of spices and the mixed vegetables. Remove from heat and set aside. Place boned pig's head into and let it be marinated for a night. Remove from marinade the follow-up day, rinse and place into a high-wall baking pan. Cover with rendered lard. Bake in oven at 175°F (80°C) for 8 hours until tender. Remove from lard and drain. Tear into pieces and place them into a casserole dish lined with plasic wrap. Cover and press down. Keep in refrigerator until serving. Serve thin sliced.

Pick off parsley leaves from stem and wash them thoroughly. Cut shallots into thin slices and sprinkle with salt carefully. Put lemon juice, mustard, honey, salt and freshly ground black pepper into a jar. Stir well, add poppy seed oil, cover and shake. Toss parsley leaves and sliced shallots and pour the vinaigrette onto.

Cut pumpkin into slices and remove pits. Bake in oven at 355°F (180°C) until tender (about 45 minutes). Peel when cool enough to handle, purée in a blender, add orange juice, oil and spices.
Serving: Spoon pumpkin purée onto thin-sliced carpaccio, place parsley salad and a few slices of smoked tongue on them. Place pickled green walnuts on the top and pour oil on it.

MANGALICA 'LIVERWURST' WITH RED CABBAGE PURÉE AND BEETROOT

INGREDIENTS (FOR 4 PERSONS):
FOR THE LIVERWURST:
4 sheets Brick or Filo pastry
14 oz / 400 g Mangalitsa liver
4 slices white bread
3/4 cup / 0.2 l milk
salt, black pepper, ground
coriander leaves
1 egg
2 shallots, medium
1/4 cup / 50 g butter

FOR THE RED CABBAGE PURÉE:
10.5 oz / 300 g red cabbage, thin sliced
1 shallot, minced
2 tbsps sugar
1 apple, peeled, grated
pinch of cumin
leaves of a sprig fresh rosemary, minced
1/2 cup / 0.1 l Frisecco sparkling wine

FOR THE GARNISHES:
1 beetroot, yellow
1 beetroot, red
1 celery root
fresh thyme
olive oil
stewed golden apple
stewed cocktail pear
2 tbsps honey
1/4 cup / 50 g butter
1 tsp Tokaj elderflower vinegar, salt

Cut liver into 1/2-inch cubes and sear on butter. Add minced shallot and coriander. Cut bread into 1/2-inch cubes, toast and soak in milk. Squeeze milk out then add bread to liver. Stir well, sprinkle with salt and ground pepper. Open Brick pastry, brush with egg, wash and fill with liver-bread mix. Roll up and brush with melted butter. Bake at 430°F (220°C) until golden brown.

Caramelize sugar on butter then add onion, cabbage and apple. Sprinkle with salt, stir well then add sparkling wine. Reduce volume, flavor with cumin and rosemary. Cook until tender, purée in a blender and stir well with butter.

Wash beetroots and celery root thoroughly and pack them separately in aluminium foil with salt, thyme and olive oil. Place them in a baking pan and bake in oven at 355°F (180°C) until tender (about 1 hour). Unpack, peel and slice vegetables. Heat butter, stir well with honey. Sauté beetroots, golden apple and pear on it then add elderflower

MILLE-FEUILLE WITH CRACKLINGS AND PLUM

INGREDIENTS (FOR 4 PERSONS):
FOR THE PASTRY:
1 pack shortcrust pastry
3.5 oz / 100 g Mangalitsa crackling

FOR THE FILLING:
7 oz / 200 g plum
1/4 cup / 60 g sugar
3.5 oz / 100 g mascarpone
1/2 cup / 0.1 l heavy cream
1.5 oz / 50 g prune

FOR THE SORBET:
10.5 oz / 300 g apricot purée
1/2 cup / 100 g sugar
1/2 cup / 0.1 l water
1 tsp / 5 g glucose
2/3 cup / 0.2 l Frisecco sparkling wine
1 tbsp / 20 ml Kecskeméti apricot pálinka
(fruit brandy)

Sprinkle shortcrust pastry with minced cracklings and roll up. Preheat oven to 410°F (210°C). Place pastry between two baking sheets and bake for 12 minutes or until crispy. Cut rounds by a circle cutter.

Caramelize sugar, add pitted plum and cook until its juice evaporates. Purée in a blender when cool enough to handle. Mix mascarpone with cream and 2 tbsps sugar then whisk until foam. Add plum purée and finely chopped prunes. Stir gently.

Put apricot purée in a pot, add sugar, glucose and water. Bring to a boil then remove from heat. Cool. Add wine and pálinka. Place it into the deep-freeze and frost it. Beat it with a whisk from time to time.

Serving: Take a pastry round and spread with filling. Put an other pastry on them and repeat layering several times. Place onto a plate and serve with wine-caramel, caramelized apricots and sorbet.

SZABOLCS DUDÁS & SZILÁRD DUDÁS

ANYUKÁM MONDTA

Although they say that their restaurant's style is Italian and their hero is a wine expert, people travel to Encs from time to time because the Dudás brothers present the culinary traditions of the Abaúj, Zemplén and Tokaj regions from a different point of view, rather than only for eating a good pizza or drinking wine.

'And how does this point of view show that region? Loose, open and fresh, just as they are.' Our hero is wine expert István Szepsy. His personality, relationship with nature, passion and expertise have had a great impact on us. He has taught us the importance of good ingredients. Here in the Anyukám Mondta Restaurant, we try to tell the story of our journey in Italy, the things we encountered and what our perception of the country is. We endeavor to work with the best of ingredients, as poor produce makes a bad dish. We try to present Abaúj, Zemplén and Tokaj through our cuisine, using local ingredients with a Mediterranean freshness. Now we are telling three stories in our three recipes. We take inspiration from the pig slaughter ceremonies from our childhood, vying for the pig's ear. Then, like now, the simple things like blood and brain were delecacies. With its high quality, versatility and uniqueness, Mangalitsa has become the iconic product of Hungarian cuisine which I'll hope you will discover in our recipes, too.'

CRISPY MANGALITSA BLOOD WITH ONION

INGREDIENTS (FOR 4 PERSONS):
4 cups / 1 l fresh Mangalitsa blood
18 oz / 500 g onion, finely chopped
2 tbsps Mangalitsa lard
1-1 tsps whole black pepper
Jamaica pepper
coriander seed
common juniper
3.5 oz / 100 g peanut, finely chopped, unsalted
36 oz / 1 kg sauerkraut (sour cabbage)
1 Savoy cabbage
salt to taste

Drain congealed blood (pour out serum) and dice. Render Mangalitsa lard and sauté onion on it. Grill spices in a nonstick pan without oil or grease then pound them in a mortar. Add blood to onion, sprinkle with spices and salt then fry it on low heat until creamy.

Steam sauerkraut. Blanch and refresh in ice cold water the outer leaves of Savoy cabbage. Cut thin stripes of the latter then mix the two types of cabbage.

Roast the finely chopped peanut in a nonstick pan. Serving: Form blood into small balls and roll them in peanuts. Serve on cabbage.

RECOMMENDED WINE
ZOLTÁN DEMETER
Tokaj Birtokbor, 2009

MANGALITSA EAR CONFIT
WITH CHICKPEA PURÉE

INGREDIENTS (FOR 4 PERSONS):
FOR THE EAR:
36 oz / 1 kg Mangalitsa ear
106 oz / 3 kg Mangalitsa lard
1 onion, finely chopped
1 bulb garlic

FOR THE CHICKPEA PURÉE:
9 oz / 250 g chickpea, cooked
1 tbsp tahini (sesame seed pasta)
2 tbsps olive oil
1 tbsp lemon juice
1 clove of garlic, grated
pinch of salt

FOR THE DECORATION:
olive oil dots
1 bunch of parsley
garlic salt

Put onion quarters in a baking pan with washed ears. Cover with lard and confit for 2.5-3 hours long in oven at 195°F (90°C) until tender.

Purée all ingredients in a blender. Serving: Fry Mangalitsa ears in a pan and garnish with chickpea purée. Make spice oil from parsley leaves, garlic salt and olive oil then pour it on the ears. You can also serve it with a gravy made of pork bones and vegetables. Sprinkle with salt grains.

RECOMMENDED WINE
SZEPSY WINE CELLAR
Furmint, 2009

MANGALITSA BRAIN WITH TRIPE

INGREDIENTS (FOR 4 PERSONS):

36 oz / 1 kg tripe, trimmed

18 oz / 500 g Mangalitsa brain

2 onions

2 cloves of garlic

2 bay leaves, whole

1 celery stalk, finely chopped

1 carrot, finely chopped

10.5 oz / 300 g tomato, peeled, diced

6-8 tbsps olive oil

1.5 tbsps / 20 g butter

3/4 cup / 0.2 l dry furmint (white wine)

2 cups / 0.5 l beef stock

salt, ground black pepper

Soak brain in water for 30 minutes then remove membranes and cut it into pieces. Cook tripe in a large pot of water with one whole onion and garlic for one hour. Drain tripe and cut into thin slices.

Blend olive oil and butter in a pan and sauté the other onion (finely chopped), carrot and celery (that is the so-called soffritto). Place tripe stripes in it, cover with wine then add tomato and beef stock. Flavor with salt and pepper. Bring to a boil then place to a baking pan. Bake in oven at 300°F (150°C) for 3 hours until tender. In the last hour add brain to it and cook to doneness. Serve with fresh bread or pita.

RECOMMENDED WINE
SZENT TAMÁS WINE CELLAR
Hárslevelű, 2011

ANTONIO FEKETE

SALON RESTAURANT

Antonio Fekete is said to be the one of the most ambitious and talented cooks of his generation. When we look through his refined and precise recipes, there is no doubt that he has a very promising career. He pays particular attention to the presentation of his dishes. 'It is important that a dish is as pleasing to the eye as it is to the palate'. Antonio Fekete was brave enough to create an apple dessert which you can see some pages later.

'My main principle is quality which I adhere to despite any difficulties. I avoid mediocrity in both my work and personal life. In cooking, harmony is just as importantt as quality – a dish must both taste and look good. When a savory dish is presented well, the guest will remember my creation for a long time.At the moment, the quality of ingredients is the main problem with Hungarian cuisine, although in many cases, for example with Mangalitsa, this has to be the most important factor to look at. If I work with this well-kept, well-bred, well-slaughtered meat, I can create some marvelous things, which I hope will lead to an increase in its popularity and be an inspiration for more breeders to get involved.'

COLD TOMATO SOUP
WITH MANGALITSA HAM

INGREDIENTS (FOR 4 PERSONS):
FOR THE SOUP:
32 oz / 900 g Lucullus tomato
5 oz / 150 g fresh raspberry
2/3 cup / 0.15 l water
1/2 cup / 100 g sugar

FOR THE SOUP TOPPER
(dried tomato):
18 oz / 500 g tomato
salt, sugar to taste
1 clove of garlic, thin sliced
1 sprig fresh thyme
olive oil

FOR THE SOUP TOPPER
(yellow tomato):
4 yellow cherry tomatoes
1 1/3 cups / 0.3 l syrup

FOR THE GREEN PASTA:
1 3/4 cups / 250 g white flour
1 egg
3 egg yolks
pinch of salt
1/2 cup / 0.1 l water
2/3 cup / 0.2 l olive oil
9 oz / 250 g spinach

FOR THE SERVING:
2 oz / 60 g Mangalitsa ham, smoked, fried
core of 1 zebra tomato
Sakura Mix mixed salad

Put tomato and raspberry in a blender and purée with sugar, salt and water to taste. Put a pan under a sieve lined with cheesecloth and pour purée in it. Place in the refreigerator and cool it for 2-3 hours. The transparent tomato soup (see our photo) will drop slowly.

Preheat oven to 100-120°F. Boil a pot of water. Cut an X on the bottom of the tomatoes. Submerge them in boiling water for 30 seconds then remove with a slotted spoon and peel away the skin. Core them and quarter. Transfer them to a baking pan lined with greaseproof paper. Flavor with salt and sugar. Cut garlic into paper-thin slices and place a slice on each piece of tomato. Sprinkle with thyme. Dry tomatoes in the oven until they lose 65-70% of water and look like dried tomatoes you buy in supermarkets. Remove garlic and thyme. Cut tomatoes into tiny cubes and pour oil on them.

Cut an X on the bottom of cherry tomatoes. Submerge them in boiling water for 30 seconds then remove with a slotted spoon and peel away the skin. Place them into the syrup. Keep cool until serve.

Wash spinach leaves thoroughly, scald them then mince. Combine spinach and the other ingredients well. Roll to thin, cut into sheets and cook to doneness in boiling water. You can cut the letters from the done pasta with alphabet cutter.

Cut thin slices from Mangalitsa ham and place in the bowls with other soup toppers. Ladle soup on them.

MANGALITSA TENDERLOIN WITH BABY VEGETABLES AND PURÉES

INGREDIENTS (FOR 4 PERSONS):
FOR THE TENDERLOIN:
22 oz / 600 g Mangalitsa tenderloin
1/2 cup / 0.1 l olive oil
1/4 cup / 50 g butter

FOR THE ZUCCHINI PURÉE:
18 oz / 500 g zucchini, cored, diced
1 clove of garlic, thin sliced
1/2 cup / 0.1 l heavy cream
1 shallot, sliced
1/4 cup / 50 g butter
sugar to taste

FOR THE JERUSALEM ARTICHOKE PURÉE:
14 oz / 400 g Jerusalem artichoke
1/4 cup / 50 ml milk
1/2 cup / 50 ml heavy cream
3/4 cup / 0.2 l vegetable stock
1/4 cup / 50 g butter

FOR THE BABY VEGETABLES:
11 oz / 300 g baby vegetable
12 brown Clamshell mushrooms
1/4 cup / 50 g butter

FOR THE GRAVY:
180 oz / 5 kg chicken back
54 oz / 1.5 kg mixed vegetables
1/2 star anise
thyme, black pepper, bay leaves to taste

Preheat oven to 375°F (190°C). Trim fat and membranes from tenderloin. Season with salt and pepper then sear in a pan. Place pan into the oven and bake for 5-8 minutes (time depends on the thickness of meat). Take meat out of oven and let rest for 5 minutes then fry it in hot butter.

Blanch and refresh zucchini dices. Boil cream, add garlic and shallot. Cook for 2 minutes then purée in a blender with zucchini. Sprinkle with salt and sugar to taste. Combine with cold butter before serving. Peel and dice Jerusalem artichoke. Cook in a pot of water with other ingredients until tender. Flavor with salt (if needed) then purée in blender. Combine with cold butter before serving, it will make it softer.

Blanch and refresh baby vegetables in ice cold water. Heat them on hot butter before serving.

Bake chicken backs in oven at 425°F (220°C) for 20 minutes. Put them into a pot and cover with cold water. Bring to a boil and skim off the scump (gravy will be cleaner and tastier). Bake vegetables and spices in oven at 425°F (220°C) for 10 minutes, then add them to chicken. Cook for 1.5-2 hours. Drain then simmer it until gets dark, oily liquid. Skim off the scump time to time. This is the base of the gravy. Combine with cold butter before serving and flavor to taste, stirring constantly.

RECOMMENDED WINE
PÓSTA WINE HOUSE
Szekszárdi Kadarka, 2009

APPLE DESSERT WITH CINNAMON

INGREDIENTS (FOR 4 PERSONS):
FOR THE CAPSULES:
4 white chocolate capsules
1.9 oz / 50 g Crème Anglaise
16 dark chocolate pearls

FOR THE APPLE MOUSSE:
3 egg yolks
1/4 cup / 45 g sugar
7 oz / 187 g whipped cream
(cca. 2/3 cup / 0.2 l cream)
1/4 cup / 45 g green apple purée (1 green apple
and 3 basil leaves puréed in a blender, drained)
1 1/2 gelatin leaves

FOR THE CRUMBS:
1 oz / 25 g Bienetta
3/4 cup / 125 g almond flour
9 oz / 250 g dried apple
pinch of cinnamon

FOR THE APPLE JELLY:
2 cups / 0.5 l water
0.1 oz / 3 g green Glanz Klar (food coating jelly)
0.2 oz / 5 g basil
0.2 oz / 5 g green apple skin

FOR THE DECORATION:
5 fresh basil leaves, small
2 oz / 50 g dark chocolate
pinch of cinnamon
7 oz / 0.2 l verjuice

RECOMMENDED WINE
HUNGÁRIA
Irsai Olivér Champagne

(Crème Anglaise: Mix 2 cups milk with 12 egg yolks over a pot of lightly boiling water, stirring constantly. Add 3/4 cup sugar and the seeds of Vanilla bean and warm. Keep egg yolks raw). Spoon the half of the Crème Anglaise into a decorating bag and fill the halves of capsules with it. Put 4 pearls in each capsule and cover with Crème Anglaise.

Soak gelatin leaves in water then warm up. Beat egg yolks with sugar, add apple purée, whipped cream and gelatin leaves. Fill the mousse into the halves of the round molds. Put the white chocolate capsules in the center. Cover with the other halves of molds and fill them with mousse. Place them in the deep-freeze.

Preheat oven to 340°F (170°C). Combine all ingredients and pat onto a greaseproof paper-lined baking sheet. Bake it until golden brown and let cool. Break it by hands and form crumbs into 4 rounds.

Purée basil and green apple skin in a blender. Add coating jelly and warm up. Dip cold balls in it.

Dry basil leaves in a hot, dry place. Temper chocholate and flavor with cinnamon. Pour it into strands on a greaseproof paper. Remove set chocolate from paper. Serving: Transfer balls, 'apples' on crumb rounds. Place apple leaves and stems onto them. Reduce verjuice until gets oily consistency then cool. Decorate plates with verjuice dots.

LÁSZLÓ JAHNI

KISTÜCSÖK

Fish from Lake Balaton is an eternal favorite for László Jahni. A wild carp is a renewed inspiration for him, as is nature and the changing of the seasons. He uses regional flavors and ingredients in the legendary Kistücsök restaurant and he likes to keep things simple. He has no idols. 'Why' he asks. 'That wouldn't be honest.'

'The Carpathian Basin with its diversity and history has passed a beautiful legacy to us. Great ingredients, recipes and cooking techniques, many of which now, unfortunately, forgotten. We must use Hungarian ingredients more and with the help of specialists, teach the world how to use them. This is what we try to do in the kitchen of the Kistücsök Restaurant. We, Hungarians like these traditional flavors but would like to develop and use them in a new way. I love using Mangalitsa meet because of its high quality and full fat content, which makes it taste so good. This has inspired me to write the recipes I have done and hope that my passion for fine food, correctly prepared will inspire you to experiment too.'

MANGALITSA LIVER PÂTÉ

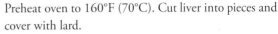

INGREDIENTS (FOR 4 PERSONS):

14 oz / 400 g Mangalitsa liver
7 oz / 200 g Mangalitsa lard
4 oz / 120g smoked Mangalitsa bath chap
1 onion, sliced
2 cloves of garlic
5-6 sprigs fresh marjoram
36 oz / 1 kg Mangalitsa skin, leg and bones
salt, freshly ground black pepper

Preheat oven to 160°F (70°C). Cut liver into pieces and cover with lard.

Add onion, garlic and bake it for 15-20 minutes. Liver should have a small amount of pink in the center. Remove liver from lard. Purée the two thirds of liver in a blender with the half of lard. Sieve. Dice the leftover liver and bath chap. Combine them with the pâté, flavor with salt, pepper and marjoram.

In case you want to slice it, cook a stock from bones, legs and skin. Drain and reduce until thick then blend with the pâté. Pour into a greased casserole dish and cool.
Serving: Sliced, with bread, pickles or lettuce salad.

RECOMMENDED WINE
KONYÁRI WINE CELLAR
Szárhegy, 2011

MANGALITSA SNACK

INGREDIENTS (FOR 4 PERSONS):

7 oz / 200 g Mangalitsa skin
7 oz / 200 g dried fruit
1 lemon juice
Maldon salt
Sunflower oil

Cook skin in a large pot of salty water with lemon juice. Cool. Roll on and cut into thin slices. Fry in deep oil until golden brown. Mind spattering hot oil! Drain on paper towel then mix with dried fruits and salt grains.

It is delicious as a snack or as a topping/ingredient for desserts as well. If you break it coarsely it can be used for breading as well. Change proportion of ingredients depending on preparing a sweet or salty dish.

RECOMMENDED WINE
KISLAKI WINE MANUFACTURE
Lakitető Syrah, 2011

MANGALITSA NECK
WITH SAVOY CABBAGE STEW

INGREDIENTS (FOR 4 PERSONS):

29 oz / 800 g Mangalitsa chuck, boneless

1 tbsp Mangalitsa lard

1 sprig fresh rosemary

1-2 sprigs fresh marjoram

1 Savoy cabbage, small

2 cups / 0.5 l vegetable stock

2 tbsps / 20 g butter

4 potatoes

salt

cumin

freshly ground black pepper to taste

oil or fat for frying

Preheat oven to 425°F (220°C). Season spare rib with salt and pepper. Place rosemary on the top and truss. Transfer in a baking pan, spread with lard and bake in oven for 5 minutes, then turn over and bake for an additional 5 minutes. Remove meat from oven. Cool oven to 240°F (110°C) and put the meat back and bake for 30 minutes. Spare rib can be grilled in open air with almost the same technique. Grill slices over big flame then let them rest at a lukewarm place.

Get off the outer green leaves. Blanch and refresh them in ice cold water. Chop the leftover cabbage and cook in vegetable stock. Season with salt, black pepper, marjoram and cumin then purée in a blender. Thicken with cold butter. Cut outer leaves into slices and mix with the purée. Dice potatoes and fry them in deep fat or oil. Serving: place spare rib slices on plates with Savoy cabbage and potatoes.

RECOMMENDED WINE
LÉGLI
Gesztenyés Rajnai Rizling, 2009

TIBOR JÁSZAI

PRÍMÁS PINCE

Tibor Jászai's ideal was eating good, refined and innovative food in Esztergom and he followed those goals to the Prímás Pince Restaurant, where he uses local produce almost exclusively. He is inspired by the dairy products of Pilismarót, honey from Esztergom, game from Szob, the Mangalitsa from Kosd, the apricot jam from Muzsla and other local products.

'One of the best things about Hungarian cuisine, generally speaking, is that we can be considered to be the larder of Europe. We have tasty fruit and vegetables, lucscious mushrooms, our grazing cattle, our berries, aspargus from Tengelic and our wines could be mentioned as our trump cards. If I can, I like to use locally sourced Hungarian ingredients. Our local specialities include carp of Szob with its red and crunchy flesh, the sweet tasting cheese by Rétki Gábor aged for six months, duck from Leléd and of course the Mangalitsa. As my family breeds Mangalitsa, I have experienced first hand the quality product resulting from good breeding practices. I love the the unique quality of this meat, its peculiar smell with the ham's specific flavor and the taste of the sausages. It also doesn't need salting or flavoring like other pork. The meat is never dry and always juicy. I love to offer the best to my guests – and that is Mangalitsa amongst pork.'

95

PRESSED DUCK LIVER WITH ZANDER AND MICRO SALADS WITH CITRUS EXTRACT

INGREDIENTS (FOR 4 PERSONS):
FOR THE LIVER:
14 oz / 400 g fat duck liver
cca. 1 cup / 0.2-0.3 l milk
1 tsp icing sugar
pinch of red paprika powder
salt, ground white pepper to taste
cca. 1 cup / 0.2-0.3 l Szent Tamás Cuvée from Tokaj (sweet white wine)

FOR THE ZANDER:
2 zander fillets, whole, skinless
(cca. 14 oz / 400-500 g)
salt, freshly ground green pepper to taste
fresh dill
zest of 1 quarter lemon
pinch of agar-agar

FOR THE MICRO SALADS AND CITRUS EXTRACT:
2-3 pinches of Sakura mix microsalad mix
2 lemons
2 limes
1 orange
4 tbsps grape seed oil

RECOMMENDED WINE
JÁSDI WINE CELLAR
Ranolder white wine, 2006

Clean off liver's veins and cut into large pieces. Put it into a bowl and cover with milk. Cover and put in the refrigerator for a night. Drain and pat dry the follow-up day. Preheat oven to 160°F (70°C). Add spices and wine then warm liver to 85°F (30°C) (simply place liver by hot oven), it helps flavors infuse deeper. Arrange liver into a casserole dish and steam it in 160°F steam oven. If you don't have steam oven: pour hot water into a baking pan until its filled half way. Place casserole dish in it and bake it for 15 minutes at 210°F (100°C). Let it rest for an hour then press down and cool.

Cut zander fillets into 1.5-inch stripes. Mince the leftover zander flesh (which had been cut off) then combine with spices and agar-agar. Spread zander fillets with this filling then cover with an other fish fillet. Repeat layering process. You may put blanched vegetables between layers on demand. Wrap in foil or place it into a loaf pan. Steam for 10 minutes at 205°F (95°C) to doneness (or cook in boiling water for 5 minutes). Cool and put in the refrigerator for a night.

Wash micro salads thoroughly and pat dry. Zest citrus peels, squeeze out their juice. Drain citrus juice and bring to a boil. Reduce by half and cool. Add citrus zests and grape seed oil then blend.

Serving: Place a slice of liver and a slice of pâté on each plate and garnish with micro salads and citrus extract. If you want to use the leftover liver or fish: form liver into balls and dredge in almond slices or dredge fish pieces in breadcrumbs and serve them as garnishes.

CIGAR-SMOKED TENDERLOIN
WITH CALF'S FEET AND ONION JAM
AND TOMATO COMPOTE

INGREDIENTS (FOR 4 PERSONS):
FOR THE TENDERLOIN:
42 oz / 1-1.2 kg Mangalitsa tenderloin
1/2 cup / 0.1 l red wine
2 sprigs thyme
2 cinnamon sticks
1 bunch of parsley
1 sprig rosemary
1 cigar, small, thin
salt, black pepper to taste

FOR THE CALF'S FEET:
2 calf's feet
bay leaf, garlic to taste
salt, black pepper seeds, whole
1 lemon, juice and zest
2 bunches of parsley, finely chopped
flour, egg and breadcrumbs for breading
grape seed oil for frying
1 carrot, cooked, thin sliced
1 celery root, small, cooked, thin sliced
1 zucchini, blanched, sliced

FOR THE ONION JAM (36 OZ):
18 oz / 500 g shallot, minced
1 star anise
1 cup / 200 g brown sugar
8 cups / 2 l red wine

FOR THE TOMATO:
12 cherry tomatoes
half bunch of rosemary
thyme
basil
1 tsp muscovado sugar
1/4 cup / 50 ml olive oil

Sprinkle meat with salt and pepper then sear in a pan. Add wine before the end of searing then set aside. Put spices and the half-burned cigar into a wine box. Place tenderloin on them. Wrap in aluminium foil and bake in oven at 350°F (180°C) for 15 minutes. Meat should have a small amount of pink in the center.

Cook feet in a large pot of water with bay leaf, garlic, salt and pepper. Bone one foot out, mince and add parsley, lemon zest, juice and a small amount of water. Combine well and pat into a pan to 1-inch thickness. Put in the refrigerator for a night. Cut it into slices, bread and fry in deep oil. Spices and seeds can be added to breadcrumbs to taste. Layer the other foot (still warm) with the carrot, celery root and zucchini. Press down and cool. Serve thin sliced.

Caramelize brown sugar and mix onion in it. Add star anise, salt, pepper and wine and cook for 3-4 hours over low heat until thicken.

Boil a pot of water. Cut an X on the bottom of the tomatoes. Submerge them in boiling water for 30 seconds then remove with a slotted spoon and peel away the skin. Spread with sugar and bake for 10 minutes in oven at 120°F (50°C). When done, pour oil on it and sprinkle with freshly chopped spices. Let it rest for a night. Serving: Place smoked tenderloin by breaded foot, layered foot, onion jam and three tomatoes on a plate.

RECOMMENDED WINE
VICA WINE CELLAR
Szekszárdi Cabernet Franc, 2009

SALTED CARAMEL SOUFFLÉ WITH PISTACHIO ICE CREAM AND ROSÉ SPRITZER SORBET

INGREDIENTS (FOR 4 PERSONS):

FOR THE SOUFFLÉ:
2/3 cup / 0.15 l milk
1 tbsp / 15 g butter
3 egg yolks
1/2 cup / 60 g flour
6 egg whites

FOR THE CARAMEL:
1/3 cup / 85 g sugar
2 tbsps / 25 g butter

FOR THE CRACKNEL:
1/3 cup / 75 g sugar
1/3 cup / 30 g almond, sliced

FOR THE SORBET:
1 orange
4 cups / 1 l rosé wine
1 cinnamon stick
4 cloves
1 1/4 cups / 250 g sugar
2 oz / 50 g glucose syrup

FOR THE ICE CREAM:
4 cups / 1 l milk
16 egg yolks
1 1/2 / 300 g cups sugar
1 Vanilla bean
16 oz / 400 g pistachio

Bring milk to a boil. Cream butter with a pinch of salt then add egg yolks, milk and the sifted flour. Drain then reduce over medium heat. Mix in a blender with caramel (prep of caramel: melt sugar without stirring then mix with butter). Beat egg whites until stiff then add to the soufflé.

Preheat the oven to 400°F (200°C). Melt sugar without stirring and add almonds. Pour into a pan and let cool. Break when solid. Line soufflé molds with cracknels and spoon pastry in them. Bake in oven for 20 minutes. Dust with icing sugar before serving.

Supreme orange. Bring wine to a boil with spices, sugar and orange flesh. Boil it then pour another quantity of soda. Add glusoce syrup then put in the refrigerator.

Combine milk, egg yolks, sugar and the seeds of Vanilla bean in a pan over a pot of lightly boiling water. Stir until thicken. Chop pistachio coarsely and add to cream. Keep in the deep-freeze and put it out only a few minutes before serving.

RECOMMENDED WINE
FRITTMANN WINERY
Blaufränkisch Rosé, 2013

MARIANN KISS

CONSULATE GENERAL OF HUNGARY, NEW YORK

Mariann Kiss owes a lot to her parents. As they encouraged her to go away for the holidays, she spent a lot of time with her grandparents who lived in the Great Hungarian Plain. This is where she first encountered the Mangalitsa 'They were big with red curly hair and strange ears – I didn't understand why they wore such huge fur coats in summer and winter!' This chef to the Consulate General of Hungary used to help out in the kitchen at pig-slaughter ceremonies in her grand-parents' house. 'I was the child who was under everybody's feet, but equally, I was the one who went to the table first and gobbled everything.'

'Today's Hungarian culinary culture is a result of a 1000 years development. Our country has good natural conditions with expertise in traditional livestock farming, fruit and vegetable growing and manufacture. We have also had the influence of the Asian nomad, German, Italian, Slavonic, Turkish, Austrian and French cuisine. This makes Hungarian cuisine rich in flavors and allows it to be competitive internationally. I prefer to use Hungarian produce, oven-baked bread, honey, soups, fresh vegetable stews and the Mangalitsa. I love working with it and use every part from head to tail, although we have to keep in mind that its greatest qualities, its marbling, richness in unsaturated fats appear only as a result of good farming. This way Mangalitsa could be. be a premium product which offers a quality experience to the consumer. The meat is tender and crispy and I'm not surprised that the world famous Serrano ham is made from it.'

SOUP DUET IN TWO COLORS

INGREDIENTS (FOR 4 PERSONS):
FOR THE POTATO CREAM SOUP:
10.5 oz / 300 g potato, peeled, diced
3 oz / 80 g mixed vegetables (shallot, leek, celery root, fennel), peeled, diced
1/4 cup / 50 ml white wine
2 cups / 0.5 l poultry stock or water
1/4 cup / 60 ml brown butter
1 tbsp dried chervil or 1/2 bunch of fresh chervil
2 tbsps lactose-free sour cream
white balsamic vinegar
salt, ground white pepper, nutmeg, bay leaves to taste

FOR THE LETCHO SOUP:
7 oz / 200 g onion, finely chopped
15 oz / 400 g tomato, peeled, sliced
7 oz / 200 g bell pepper, diced
22 oz / 600 g sweet pepper, diced
2 oz / 50 g smoked side bacon, minced
2 tbsps sunflower oil
2 tbsps cream
salt, black pepper, marjoram to taste

FOR THE SERVING:
7 oz fat goose liver | 20 dkg
4 slices Mangalitsa ham (three-month old)

Fry potatoes and vegetables in shallow fat then cover with wine. Reduce by two third. Add vegetable stock and spread with spices to taste then cook until tender over medium heat. Remove bay leaves and purée the leftover in a blender. Drain then add sour cream, spices and vinegar to taste. If it is too thick, add some water or stock in addition. Bring to a boil. Add brown butter only few minutes before serving. (Prep of brown butter: Melt butter over low heat which allows butter to separate into butterfat and milk solids. The milk solids naturally sink to the bottom of the pan and, if left over gentle heat, will begin to brown.)

Boil a pot of water. Cut an X on the bottom of the tomatoes. Submerge them in boiling water for 30 seconds then remove with a slotted spoon and peel away the skin. Cut them into segments. Wash paprikas, remove stems, ovaries and seeds then slice. Cut peeled onion into thin slices. Fry minced bacon on oil over medium heat. Sauté onion on bacon fat then add pepper dices and toss together with onion. Cook for 10 minutes over medium heat. Add tomatoes then flavor with salt, ground pepper and a pinch of marjoram. It must be more watery than traditional letcho. Purée in a blender, sieve and thicken with cream.

Serving: Ladle about 2/3 cup of letcho soup into bowls first, then pour a little potato soup (about 1/2 cup into the center). Cut goose liver into four slices and roast in a pan over medium heat. Fry ham slices until crunchy. Garnish soup bowls with liver and ham slices. You can offer grissini as a garnish as well.

RECOMMENDED WINE
TIBOR GÁL
VRC (Viognier-Riesling Cuvée), 2006

HOCK TARTARE WITH CRESS

INGREDIENTS (FOR 4 PERSONS):
FOR THE HOCK TARTARE:
18 oz / 500 g Mangalitsa hock
54 oz / 1.5 kg Mangalitsa lard
1 sprig rosemary
2 sprigs thyme
3 sprigs marjoram
1 bay leaf, whole
3 cloves of garlic

FOR THE QUAIL EGGS:
2 oz / 50 g trout caviar
6 quail eggs
1 anchovy, small
zest of 1/2 lemon
1 tbsp homemade mayonnaise
1 tbsp lactose-free sour cream

FOR THE VINAIGRETTE:
1/4 cup / 60 ml white balsamic vinegar
1 tbsp sherry
1 tbsp Dijon whole-grain mustard
1 tbsp Dijon hot mustard
4 scallions, finely chopped
4 pickled cucumbers, finely chopped
3/4 cup / 0.2 l extra virgin olive oil
2 tbsps fresh cress
salt, freshly ground green pepper
icing sugar to taste

FOR THE GARLIC:
8 cloves of garlic
cca. 1 cup / 0.1-0.2 l milk
1/4 cup / 50 ml olive oil or sunflower oil

Make a marinade from all ingredients except lard. Soak hock in marinade for 24 hours. Pat dry and sear, then transfer into a pan with thicker walls. Cover with rendered lard and bake in oven at 175°F. Poke a toothpick into the hock. When it slides in with no resistance you have a done meat. It takes about 3-4 hours. Heat oven to 430°F (220°C). Bake hock in oven until skin is crunchy. Remove skin and fat when cool enough to handle and cut hock into tiny cubes. Cook quail eggs and peel. Cut into halves. Combine mayonnaise with sour cream, anchovy, lemon zest and the hard boiled egg yolks. Flavor with salt and pepper. Spoon back into the egg whites. Place some caviar on the top and put in the refrigerator.

Blend vinegar, sherry and the two types of mustard with a whisk then add sugar and salt. Spoon oil into the mixture, stirring constantly. It has to be creamy. Add scallions and cucumber. Mix well, sprinkle with spices to taste. Add cress at the end and let it rest for 10 minutes.

Boil a pot of cold water with the peeled garlic cloves. Drain then cover garlic cloves with cold milk. Bring to a boil again and cook for about 5 minutes (they must be crunchy but tender). Drain and pat dry, then fry in oil until golden brown.

Serving: Mix the half of minced hock with the half of the vinaigrette. Form rounds. Place a quail egg on the top. Garnish with vinaigrette and garlic cloves. Serve with toast.

RECOMMENDED WINE
VILLA TOLNAY
Csobánci Bandérium, 2006

MANGALITSA CHOP WITH TRUFFLED PORK BELLY

INGREDIENTS (FOR 4 PERSONS):
FOR THE CHOP:
4 slices Mangalitsa chop with bones
36 oz / 1 kg Mangalitsa lard
2 sprigs thyme
2 sprigs marjoram
3 cloves of garlic
4 slices truffled pork belly

FOR THE MINCED CALF LIVER:
7 oz / 200 g calf liver
1 onion, finely chopped
2 cloves of garlic
1-2 bay leaves
1 tbsp black pepper, whole
2 oz / 50 g chanterelle
2 oz / 50 g button mushroom, brown
2 scallions, small
2 tbsps grape seed oil
4 quail eggs
breadcrumbs, gluten-free
salt, freshly ground black pepper
2-3 sprigs fresh thyme
1/2 tbsp fresh parsley

FOR THE TENDERLOIN:
18 oz / 500 g Manglica tenderloin
2 oz / 50 g amaranth
3.5 oz / 100 g quinoa
6 Savoy cabbage leaves
2 oz / 50 g pine nut
1/2 cup / 0.1 l heavy cream, lactose-free
salt, freshly ground black pepper
vinegar (10%)
ground nutmeg flower

Marinate chop slices in 6% brine for 3 days then rinse thoroughly in tap water. Transfer into a baking pan, cover with lard, add spices and confit in oven at 175°F (80°C). Heat oven to 355°F (180°C). Pat chop dry, cover with truffled pork belly slices and bake to doneness. Bring to a boil a pot of water with the liver, bay leaves, black pepper, onion and garlic. Simmer it for a while then cool. Cut into small dices. Wash chanterelles and button mushrooms thoroughly in tap water. Pat dry and chop. Sauté scallions on oil. Add liver and sear for 2 minutes. Add chanterelles, mushrooms, salt, pepper and thyme leaves. Mix well and cook until mushrooms' juice evaporates then let cool. Add eggs and breadcrumbs, combine well. Flavor to taste. Form pastry into 1.5-inch rounds and fry them in grape seed oil. Wash quinoa well in tap water in a fine mesh strainer. Put twice as much water to volume of quinoa in a pan, bring to a boil and cook quinoa for 25 minutes. Wash Savoy cabbage leaves well and blanch them in boiling salty water with vinegar (20 seconds). Refresh in ice cold water and drain then cut into thin slices. Sauté on shallow fat then add to quinoa. Toast pine nuts in a nonstick pan and add to the quinoa as well. Add cream and flavor with spices. Sprinkle tenderloin with salt and black pepper. Brush with grape seed oil and set aside for 20 minutes. Sear all sides in a pan. The center of the meat has to be done as well but shouldn't be dry! Cover with plastic foil and let it rest for 5-10 minutes. Cut into 4 slices and dredge them into amaranth seeds. Add cream and butter to the dripping and heat, that is the gravy. Serve with polenta.

RECOMMENDED WINE
MAURUS
*Rejtelem Chardonnay
(Mystery Chardonnay), 2008*

ZSOLT LITAUSZKI

21 HUNGARIAN KITCHEN

Although he is still young man, Zsolt Litauszki has had a very exciting background. He travelled extensively to the best restaurants in Austria to climb the ladder of success. When they didn't want to let him go from the Michelin starred restaurant Taubenkobel, it was already visible that he was destined to become one of the best chefs in Hungary. As soon as he came home, he led the restaurants Pest-Buda, 21 and Pierrot.

'I have worked a lot in abroad and now we have a lot of tourists *(21 Hungarian Kitchen is located in the Buda Castle - editor's remark)*, and I faced that Hungarian cuisine was not well known out there. There are some magic words of course – e.g. goulash - which sounds familiar to everyone, but it would be much better if we could give a more complex picture of us and our cuisine, using the unique qualities of the Carpathian Basin. Hungarian ingredients, such as the Mangalitsa are dominant in my kitchen. It has good taste and consistency, but it is also important where it comes from – so I love it because it has a Carpathian origin. I am primarily inspired by the smell, color and consistency of food and my goal is to cook high quality dishes from high quality ingredients. That's why my dishes are simple, rather than complicated. I love working with offals. I created a main dish of Mangalitsa tongue, because I find it very exciting. I was wondering how would a sweet dessert taste with Mangalitsa lard, so I tried it, and I am satisfied with the result.'

MANGALITSA RILLETTE IN BREADCRUMBS WITH FERMENTED WAX BEANS

INGREDIENTS (FOR 4 PERSONS):
FOR THE RILLETTE:
7 oz / 200 g Mangalitsa bacon
11 oz / 300 g Mangalitsa shoulder
4 oz / 125 g Mangalitsa fat
2 tbsps white wine
1 1/4 / 0.3 l cups stock
pinch of salt / 8 g
0.3 oz / 1 g white pepper, whole
1 bay leaf, whole
1 sprig thyme
1 sprig parsley
1/8 star anise
1 egg
4 tbsps / 20 g flour
2 oz / 50 g sourdough bread
3/4 cup / 0.2 l sunflower oil

FOR THE WAX BEANS:
1 cup / 0.25 l lukewarm water
9 oz / 250 g wax bean
1 sprig dill
1 clove of garlic
1 grape leaf
1 oz / 25 g sourdough bread

FOR THE SERVING:
1.5 oz / 40 g mixed salad
1 tbsp verjuice
1 tsp Dijon mustard
pinch of sugar

Put all ingredients into a jar with 2-3 tbsps salt. Allow them to fregment at a sunny, warm place to doneness.

Cut bread into thin slices, dry and shred.

Render Mangalitsa fat over medium heat. Add meats and green spices then simmer uncovered for 1 hour, stirring constantly. Add salt and pepper. Cover with liquids and simmer covered for 4 hours over low heat. Drain and cool. Skim fat and set aside. Pull apart the fibres with a fork then combine with dripping and fat in order to get a thick, formable pastry. Chill in refrigerator and slice. Bread slices in flour, egg then sourdough breadcrumbs and fry in deep fat.

Blend all ingredients of the dressing. Add a pinch of salt and one tbsp ice cold water. Toss dressing with lettuce leaves. Serving: Place beans on plates first, cover with salads. Put rillette on the top.

RECOMMENDED WINE
KERTÉSZ FAMILY WINE CELLAR
Zöldveltelini (Green Veltliner), 2009

CRACKLING DUMPLINGS WITH MANGALITSA TONGUE, CABBAGE AND TARRAGON

INGREDIENTS (FOR 4 PERSONS):
FOR THE TONGUE:
18 oz / 500 g Mangalitsa tongue
1 small onion
2 cloves of garlic
salt
whole black pepper to taste
bay leaf

FOR THE DUMPLINGS:
9 oz / 250 g potato
2 oz / 50 g strudel flour
1 egg
1 tbsp potato starch
4 oz / 120 g Mangalitsa crackling
0.5 oz / 10 g onion
1 clove of garlic
1 sprig thyme

FOR THE CABBAGE:
11 oz / 300 g cabbage
1 tbsp / 10 g butter
0.5 oz / 10 g onion
1/4 cup / 50 ml white wine
2 cups / 0.5 l stock
salt, ground black pepper, fresh tarragon

FOR THE MANGALITSA CHIPS:
3.5 oz / 100 g Mangalitsa skin
1 oz black pepper, whole
1 bay leaf

Tongues are recommended to prepare one day earlier. Cook them with onions and spices until tender. Peel off their skin when still warm. Place them back to the cooking water and let cool.

Boil potatoes in salty water (one day earlier as well if possible), drain and cool then grate. Heat cracklings in a pan with onion and spices. Purée in a blender the one third of it, then mix with the leftover and cool. Combine potatoes with flour, starch, salt, eggs and pepper. Form pastry into balls. Push some crackling cream into balls' center. Cook them in boiling water to doneness.

Cut cabbage into thin slices then sauté with onion on butter. Flavor with salt and pepper. Pour white wine on it and reduce until all juices evaporate. Cover with stock and simmer. Season with tarragon.

Serving: Place cabbage on a plate. Put dumplings and tongue on them. Cook Mangalitsa skin in boiling water with black pepper and bay leaf until tender. Drain and purée in a blender with a small amount of cooking water. Sieve and cool in the refrigerator. Break medium-sized pieces and bake them in oven at 400°F (200°C) until crunchy. Serve Mangalitsa tongue with chips.

RECOMMENDED WINE
RÁSPI WINE CELLAR
Pinot Noir, 2005

GERBEAUD

INGREDIENTS (FOR 4 PERSONS):
FOR THE PASTRY:
2 1/2 cups / 300 g brown flour
7 oz / 200 g Mangalitsa lard
5 oz / 150 g walnut, toasted, ground
1 egg
2 egg yolks
1/4 cup / 50 g brown sugar
1 oz / 20 g yeast
pinch of salt
2 tbsps sour cream

FOR THE FILLING:
11 oz / 300 g apricot jam
7 oz / 200 g walnut, toasted, ground
7 oz / 200 g dark chocolate

FOR THE BREADED APRICOT:
3.5 oz / 100 g white chocolate
4 apricots
4 tsps / 20 ml rum
1 egg
1 tbsp flour
1/4 cup / 50 ml milk
3/4 cup / 0.2 l sunflower oil for frying

Combine all ingredients well and form 3-4 loaves from pastry. Let it rise for 30 minutes. Roll one loaf to thin and place into a baking pan.

Spread pastry with filling (apricot jam mixed with walnut). Repeat layering with the remaing pastry and filling. Pastry should be on top at the end. Bake in oven at 350°F (180°C) for 25 minutes with air circulation. Melt the chocholate over a pot of steaming water. Spread pastry with it, when the former is cool enough to handle.

Remove pits. Place white chocolate into apricots' center. Beat egg whites with a whisk until stiff. Add other ingredients. Dip apricots in this pastry and fry them in deep fat. Drain and serve as a garnish.

RECOMMENDED WINE
ATTILA WINE CELLAR
Turán, 2008

GYÖRGY LŐRINCZ

BABEL

György Lőrincz was one of the founding members of the fine-dining restaurant Babel, where he has been executive chef since its' reopening. His credo is the Guest. It means that the guest's complex experience is the most important thing for him. That is a language of flavors, mood and looks, and he wants to speak that language best in order to satisfy the guests.

'I prefer traditional cuisine, so therefore use classic ingredients. I enjoy focusing on forgotten or rarely used foods and show them as they were originally used or with a modern twist. Memories inspire me, an old flavor or smell from childhood and particularly remembering my grandma who had a great influence on my love of cooking, introducing me to the old tastes and smells. Because of its rich flavors and spices, Hungarian cuisine is quite complex. I believe it can stand side by side with French cuisine with bold and dominent full-bodied flavors. Mangalitsa is a good example of this because it's quality is consistent. It doesn't have a typical 'pork' taste. I think the world will start discovereing this forgotten treasure. That pleases me so much as Mangalitsa is good and Mangalitsa is ours!'

MANGALITSA JOWL RILLETTE WITH HOMEMADE FERMENTED VEGETABLES

INGREDIENTS (FOR 4 PERSONS):
FOR THE RILLETTE:
9 oz / 250 g bacon, diced
9 oz / 250 g Mangalitsa jowl, sliced
3.5 oz / 100 g Mangalitsa fat, diced
1-2 shallots
1-2 cloves of garlic, cut into halves
2 tbsps / 20 g Mangalitsa lard
1/2 cup / 0.1 l red wine reduction
1 1/2-2 cups / 0.3-0.5 l red wine
4-6 cups / 1-1.5 l broth or vegetable stock
2 tbsps / 40 g salt
1 tbsp sugar
freshly ground black pepper

FOR THE FERMENTED VEGETABLES:
1 portion of baby corn
1 bunch radish
8-10 pickles, medium sized
2 bunches of dill
2 tbsps / 50 g salt
2 cloves of garlic
3 slices dry bread
10-15 black pepper seeds, whole
5-10 mustard seeds
elderberry extract or elderflower

Heat fat and bacon until rendering then add meats. Cut peeled shallot into large pieces. Peel garlic and cut into halves. Add them to meats and simmer uncovered for an hour, stirring time to time. Cover with vegetable stock or broth and wine reduction. Add salt and pepper. Cover (with a little gap) and simmer over low heat for 4-6 hours. Drain and cool. Skim off the fat from dripping and trim the leftover fat pieces. Pull apart the fibres of meats and purée shallots with a fork. Put meat pan back over the heat, add the leftover dripping, a small amount of lard and sugar, stirring constantly. Remove from heat when it becomes a homogene pulp and cool. Spoon into molds.

Wash and scrub pickles thoroughly and cut the ends (it is recommended to soak pickles for 10-15 minutes in order to remove hairs easily) and put them in a jar. Place garlic cloves, dill, whole black pepper, elderberry extract or elderflower beside the pickles. Prepare the brine (add a handful of salt to each litre of water, bring to a boil and let cool to room-temperature) and cover pickles with it. Place a slice of bread on the top. Let the brine saturate bread slice.
Cover and put jar into a warm place. Repeat process with the two other vegetables. Babycorn needs no elderflower, radish needs neither dill nor elderflower! Fermentation takes some days. Drain when done. Put vegetables back to the fermented brine and cool them together in the refrigerator. Serve them with the rillette and bread.

RECOMMENDED WINE
HERNYÁK WINERY
Birtokbor, 2009

THREE TYPES OF PORK WITH PAPRIKA POTATO STEW

INGREDIENTS (FOR 4 PERSONS):

4 Mangalitsa feet

4 Mangalitsa noses

9 oz / 250 g Mangalitsa head meat

2 Mangalitsa ears

caul fat (can be replaced by baking sheet, aluminium foil)

1 carrot

10-15 black pepper seeds, whole

1 tsp sugar

2 cups / 0.5 l white wine

3.5 oz / 100 g Panko breadcrumbs

3 eggs

7 oz / 200 g duck fat

2 cups / 0.5 l olive oil

FOR THE GRAVY:

1/2 cup / 0.1 l white wine

1/2 cup / 0.1 l apple juice

1/2 - 2/3 cup / 100-150 g butter

1/2 cup / 50 ml heavy cream

18 oz / 500 g potato

1/4 cup / 50 g butter

5 shallots

5-6 cloves of garlic

2/3 - 3/4 cup / 175 ml sour cream

1 bunch of leek

2 bunches of parsley

1-2 bay leaves

2-3 tsps red paprika powder

18 oz / 500 g bacon

1 green apple

2 cloves of garlic

Place all peeled vegetables in a large pot of water with noses, head meat, feet and ears and boil. Add some salt and cook until tender then drain. It is quicker if you make it in pressure cooker. Fill noses with the half of the head meat then cool. Bread them with beated egg whites and Panko breadcrumbs then fry in deep duck fat until golden brown. Cut ears into Julienne and fry them in deep fat. Remove bones from feet, flavor to taste. Place them onto a greaseproof paper and press down. Line an oiled baking sheet with caul fat, transfer the pressed feet onto then roll up tight with aluminium foil. Cut into pieces and sear on hot shallow fat. Bake in oven at 400°F (200°C) for 8-10 minutes with air circulation. Cool and sear once more before serving. Boil the leftover dripping until thicken. Flavor with white wine and apple juice. Add some butter and cream. Soak bacon in 10 % brine for an hour, then in clear cold water twice 8 minutes. Remove from water, sprinkle with salt, pepper. Add green apple and spices then place into sous vide at 140°F (59°C) for 12 hours. It can also be prepared in fat. In that case fry it in 108 oz / 3 kg duck fat with the same spices for 4-6 hours. Cool, form to taste and sear the skinny side on hot shallow fat.

Cut some pretty potatoes into halves and cook them in salty water with butter, or fry them in deep fat. Make a stew from the leftover potatoes with garlic, bay leaves and parsley. Purée in a blender with sour cream and red paprika powder. Sprinkle with minced fresh onion. Serve with the ear, foot, bacon and gravy spots.

RECOMMENDED WINE
TORNAI WINE CELLAR
Aranyhegy Juhfark

APRICOT STRUDEL TYROLESE STYLE

INGREDIENTS (FOR 4 PERSONS):

2 cups / 250 g flour
4.5 oz / 120 g Mangalitsa fat, trimmed
1 tbsp sour cream
1 tsp vinegar
1 tsp salt
1 tsp sugar
1/8 cup / 20 ml apricot pálinka (fruit brandy)

FOR THE FILLING:

18 oz / 500 g apricot
7 oz / 200 g dried apricot, finely chopped
1 Vanilla bean
1/4 cup / 40 ml apricot pálinka (fruit brandy)
2 tbsps honey
1/2 cup / 100 g butter
1 tbsp balsamic vinegar, white

FOR THE ICE CREAM:

1 1/3 cups / 0.3 l heavy cream
3/4 cup / 0.2 l milk
3 egg yolks
3-4 tbsps sugar
1 Vanilla bean
1/4 cup / 40 ml apricot pálinka (fruit brandy)
half jar apricot jam (good quality)

FOR THE APRICOTS:

3/4 cup / 200 g butter
1/4 cup / 50 g sugar
1/2 cup / 50 g salty almond

RECOMMENDED WINE
BOZÓKY WINE CELLAR
Móri Ezerjó Aszú (6 puttonyos), 2006

Remove apricot pits. Cook 8 halves in butter and sugar then fill with almonds. Caramelize the leftover apricots in honey. Add dried apricots then flambé with pálinka. Add seeds of Vanilla bean, balsamic vinegar and cook until becomes formable.

Combine trimmed fat with 2 oz flour well and set aside for 25 minutes to a cold place. Blend the other ingredients, set aside for 15 minutes then roll out on a floured surface to about a thickness of a finger. Spread with floury fat, roll up and start lengthening in order to form a rectangular shape. When it has a width of a finger again, fold it: the lower part first, then the upper one, the right and at last the left side to the center. Pat down and set aside for 20-25 minutes in cool place. Roll out and fold again and repeat two more times. Cut long stripes after the last folding and roll them around an oily baking mold (chimney cake mold or croquembouche). Bake them in oven at 390°F for 10-15 minutes until doneness. Dust with icing sugar when still hot. Tip: Put grinded cracklings in the pastry. Reduce the quantity of fat in that case.

Boil cream with a pinch of salt and the seeds of Vanilla bean then remove from flame. Cream egg yolks with sugar then add it to the mixture, stirring constantly. Add apricot jam and pálinka. Cool then put into the deepfreeze. Frost until reaches the desired consistency. Stir it time to time.

Serving: Spoon the filling into the baked pastries. Garnish with filled apricots, ice cream and a thick gravy made from the leftover apricot jam.

KRISZTIÁN NAGY

CHIANTI RESTAURANT

Veszprém is an important spot on the Hungarian gastronomy map thanks to Krisztián Nagy, chef at the Chianti Restaurant, one of the most promosing restaurants outside of Budapest. His dishes are refined works of art, full of details, disparate flavors coming together to create beautiful harmony.

'Hungarian cuisine is going through a radical change and we have only just started taking the first few steps. We are 40-50 years behind so we have a lot of catching up to do, particularly with all the outside influences. Thankfully, a new generation of chefs is emerging who are embracing this concept. Redifining Hungarian cuisine according to demand is the challenge and in order to achieve this, co-operation with wineries, cheese makers, farmers and manufacturers is necessary. The new popularity of the Mangalitsa is very welcome. It is a result of the co-operation of breeders, traders, cooks and open-minded people devoted to good quality food. I hope Mangalitsa takes the place it deserves.'

MANGALITSA RILLETTE WITH WHEY CHEESE AND PORCINI SALAD

INGREDIENTS (FOR 4 PERSONS):
FOR THE RILLETTE:
14 oz / 400 g Mangalitsa shoulder
18 oz / 500 g Mangalitsa lard
1/2 bulb garlic
5.5 oz / 150 g whey cheese
2 spring onions
20 caper berries
1/2 bunch of parsley, finely chopped
salt
green pepper
bay leaf

FOR THE SALAD:
7 oz / 200 g porcini
1 tsp olive oil
pinch of salt
1-2 tbsps balsamic vinegar, white
1-2 tbsps truffle oil, white

FOR THE PARSLEY OIL:
1/2 bunch of parsley, finely chopped
1 clove of garlic
cca. 1/2 cup / 0.1-0.2 l olive oil

Sprinkle meat with salt and place it into a baking pan with spices. Cover with lard. Confit it at 175°F (80°C) for 5-6 hours with air circulation until tender. Cool and pull apart meat fibres with a fork. Blend with whey cheese, parsley, spring onion, caper berries and salt to taste. Cut some paper-thin slices from the meat. Line a casserole dish with transparent plastic foil and place slices on it. Spoon the pulp in the dish and cover with meat slices. Cover with plastic foil and press down. Place into the refrigerator for 2-3 hours.

Wash porcini thoroughly. Cut into pieces of the same size. Sauté on a few drops of olive oil. Cool and sprinkle with salt, then add balsamic vinegar and truffle oil. Serving: Form rillette into shapes on demand and garnish with salad. Place parsley, garlic and olive oil into a blender and purée. Pour onto the rillette and the porcini salad.

RECOMMENDED WINE
JÁSDI WINE CELLAR
Lőczedombi Szürkebarát (Pinot gris), 2011

MANGALITSA SHOULDER WITH AGED BEEF RIBS, GNOCCHI AND ROASTED TOMATO

INGREDIENTS (FOR 4 PERSONS):
FOR THE MEATS:

22 oz / 600 g Mangalitsa shoulder (thick part)

3 tbsps olive oil

6 dried tomatoes, finely chopped

30 baby spinach leaves

3-4 thin slices of pancetta (bacon)

18 oz / 500 g beef ribs

3 tbsps olive oil

3.5 oz / 100 g onion, finely chopped

3.5 oz / 100 g celery root, finely chopped

3.5 oz / 100 g carrot, sliced

1/2 bulb garlic

3 bay leaves

2 sprigs thyme

2 sprigs fresh rosemary

3/4 cup / 0.2 l vegetable stock

1 tbsp cold butter

1/4 cup / 50 ml dry red wine

1 tsp tomato purée

FOR THE GARNISHES:

14 oz / 400 g potato

1 egg

cca. 1 cup / 100 g flour

1/2 bunch of parsley

1/2 cup / 0.1 l olive oil

30 cherry tomatoes

2 bay leaves

1/2 lemon

3-4 sprigs thyme

3 cloves of garlic

cca. 3/4 cup / 0.2 l olive oil

2 tsps xylitol

Preheat oven to 175°F (80°C). Trim shoulder in order to have a nice shape then stick a thin knife into. Combine dried tomatoes, pancetta and baby spinach leaves and fill shoulder with this mixture. Truss and sear on hot olive oil. Bake it in oven for 90 minutes until 145°F (63°C) internal temperature. Take meat out from oven and let it rest. Sprinkle ribs with salt and pepper then sear. Remove from pan. Sauté celery root, carrot and onion in the same pan. Add spices, tomato purée and wine. Sauté this mixture until golden brown then place meat into it. Cover and steam until doneness. Remove meat when tender. Thicken sieved gravy with cold butter before serving.

Cook potatoes with their skins on in salty water. Peel them when they are still warm and mash. When cool enough to handle add salt, eggs and as much flour as necessary to ensure the dough is not sticking. Roll out on a floured surface to about a thickness of a finger. Cut long stripes, twist them and cut into small dumplings. Cook them in boiling salty water until dumplings come to the surface (about 2 minutes). Drain and sauté dumplings on hot oil. Flavor with parsley oil (half bunch of parsley puréed in a blender with garlic and olive oil).

Boil a pot of water. Cut an X on the bottom of the tomatoes. Submerge them in boiling water for 30 seconds then remove with a slotted spoon and peel away the skin. Heat olive oil and spices to 105°F (40°C) and confit tomatoes in it for 10-20 minutes.

Serving: Slice meats and garnish with gnocchi and tomatoes.

RECOMMENDED WINE
FRIGYES BOTT
Blaufränkisch, 2010

MANGALITSA CHOP WITH WHITE BEAN GRAVY AND SCALLOPS

INGREDIENTS (FOR 4 PERSONS):

FOR THE CHOP:

29 oz / 800 g Mangalitsa chop
2-3 tbsps olive oil
4-5 cloves of garlic
5 bay leaves
1 sprig fresh rosemary
salt, freshly ground black pepper to taste

FOR THE GRAVY:

5.5 oz / 150 g white bean
2 tbsps olive oil
1 onion, diced
1/2 celery root, diced
1 blanched celery
3 cloves of garlic
3 bay leaves
1 tbsp cold butter
1 lemon zest
1 lemongrass
2 cups / 0.5 l vegetable stock

FOR THE SCALLOPS:

4 scallops, large
1 tbsp butter
olive oil
1/2 lemongrass
zest of 1/2 lemon
4-5 lemon balm leaves
sea salt to taste

Preheat oven to 175°F. (80°C) Trim fat from meat and flavor with salt and pepper. Truss in order to have a severe shape and sear on olive oil. Place garlic, bay leaves and rosemary on the top and bake in oven for about 3 hours (until 135°F (58°C) core temperature). Meat remains pink, soft and juicy.

Soak beans in cold water a night before. Sauté onion, garlic, celery root and celery on olive oil. Add beans, cover with vegetable stock. Season with salt, bay leaves, minced lemongrass and lemon zest. Simmer until tender then purée in a blender with cold butter.

Sauté scallops on olive oil. Season with salt, minced lemongrass, lemon zest, lemon balm leaves and add a tbsp butter. This is a very quick process since scallops don't need long heat treatment. Serving: Slice meat and garnish with white bean gravy and scallops. You may decorate the plate with some leftover beans or vegetables.

RECOMMENDED WINE
SZEPSY WINE CELLAR
Furmint, 2009

PÉTER PATAKY

IKON RESTAURANT

A spritzer is a perfect choice in a hot summer afternoon, made of young, white wine or rosé... Just like wines, restaurants need time to be matured. They are smooth and green when they are young, looking for their way. But as they are getting older, they collect experiences, meet a lot of people, farmers and opinions.

IKON matured a lot. We are still strong but more tender. We went back to our roots keeping an eye on old memories. As a barrel's taste can be felt in wine, IKON asorbed all experiences and aromas of that almost three years - and we are still perfect for a hot summer afternoon...

'I was born in Tiszalök, near the Tisza river and I couldn't fancy a holiday without the River. Wherever I travelled all over the world, water was my alpha and omega, and Tisza remained my love. It has magnificent smell, beautiful colors and it is covered by misty clouds in the mornings. I always find my peace of mind at the banks of Tisza.

When I was a child I went angling with my father and grandfather. Of course we weren't always succesful, but who cares? There were raspberry or red currant bushes everywhere....

Our grandfathers told that one becomes hungry near to water - and it is true!

I had been working in the United Kingdom for 3 years and I always got at the seashore. During these years I have learned a lot. Now I work in Debrecen and I try to combine my childhood memories, foreign experiences with local foods. That Holy Trinity is my motto in my cuisine, in IKON.'

MANGALITSA HEART AND TONGUE SALAD WITH TOAST AND CRISPY SKIN

INGREDIENTS (FOR 4 PERSONS):

1 Mangalitsa tongue
1 Mangalitsa heart
Mangalitsa skin
a few slices white bread
a few capers
a few cherry tomatoes (in different colors)
extra virgin olive oil
wine vinegar
1 tsp mustard, whole-grain
honey
1 bulb garlic, crushed
1 onion, small
salt
ground black pepper
thyme
chive
bay leaf
fresh parsley

Scald tongue and heart with a mixture of boiling water and vinegar then peel tongue.

Bring a large pot of water to boil with tongue, heart, salt, garlic, bay feal, onion, thyme, freshly ground pepper and wine vinegar and cook meats to doneness.

Cool. Remove meats from cooking water and cut them into strips.

Cut skin into strips and sprinkle with salt a day before and set aside for a night.

Rinse and pat dry, then arrange skin strips in a parchment-lined baking pan. Put an other sheet of baking paper on the top and press down with an other baking pan. Bake in oven at 300°F (150°C) for 30 minutes pressed down then remove upper baking pan and bake at 355°F (180°C) for a few minutes.

Combine mustard, salt, honey, a small amount of wine vinegar and olive oil. Mix offals with that marinade and set them aside for some hours.

Cut tomatoes into halves, sprinkle with salt. Mix together with chive and parsley.

Arrange them in jars and garnish with caper and toast.

CATFISH FROM TISZA ROLLED IN MANGALITSA BACON WITH ZUCCHINI

INGREDIENTS (FOR 4 PERSONS):

22 oz / 600 g catfish fillet, thick
(from the back of fish if possible, soaked in 6%
brine for 2 hours)
a few slices Mangalitsa bacon, thin
salt, freshly ground black pepper
1 zucchini, green
1 zucchini, yellow
10.5 oz / 300 g potato, small
1.5 oz / 50 g smoked salmon
fresh dill
fresh parsley
chervil
saffron
1 lemon, juice
2/3 cup / 150 g butter
1/2 cup / 0.1 heavy cream
1/2 cup / 0.1 Chardonnay
1 shallot
3/4 cup / 0.2 fish stock

Place bacon slices on a sheet of aluminium foil. The end of a slice should cover the end of the next slice. Arrange rinsed catfish fillet on bacon crosswise.

Roll up tight, close the ends and put in the refrigerator. Heat oil in a pan and place catfish on it (in foil). Turn it in every two minutes.

Place in oven for 15-30 minutes (time depends on the size of fillets) and bake until reaches 100°F (38°C) core temperature.

Wash potatoes thoroughly, cut into halves and cook in salty water. Pat dry and sauté on hot butter. Season with ground pepper and chervil.

Cut balls from zucchini with a melon baller. Blanch and refresh them. Sauté on salty butter for a second before serving.

Bring fish stock to a boil with wine, shallot, saffron and reduce to 1/4 cup. Add ice cold butter cubes, stirring constantly. Flavor with salt, lemon juice, freshly chopped dill and salmon. Keep at room temperature until serving.

Serve catfish fillets with zucchini balls, potato and gravy.

CHOCOLATE, ORANGE AND PASSION FRUIT

INGREDIENTS (FOR 4 PERSONS):
MILK CHOCOLATE GANACHE:
1 3/4 cups / 425 g cream
18 oz / 500 g milk chocolate

BROWNIE WITH WHITE CHOCOLATE:
3/4 cup / 190 g butter
9 oz / 250 g white chocolate
1 1/4 cups / 250 g sugar
5 eggs
1 1/4 cups / 155 g white flour
pinch of salt

TRUFFEL BALLS:
7 oz / 200 g dark chocolate
4/5 cup / 200 g cream

ORANGE JELLY:
2 cups orange juice (freshly squeezed, pulp-free)
6 gelatin leaves, 1/4 cup sugar

COCOA TUILE:
3/4 cup / 150 g sugar
1/4 cup / 30 g white flour
1/4 cup / 70 ml milk
1/2 cup / 105 g butter
0.5 oz / 10 g cocoa powder

PASSION FRUIT PURÉE:
2 cups / 0.5 l passion fruit purée
3/4 cup / 150 g sugar
3 gelatin leaves

Milk chocolate ganache: temper chocolate over a pot of lightly boiling water. Bring cream to a boil then mix with melted chocolate in two portions. Spoon 2 oz chocolate cream in each glass.

Brownie with white chocolate: preheat oven to 340°F (170°C). Melt white chocolate and butter over a pot of lightly boiling water. Beat eggs with sugar and salt then add sieved flour, stirring constantly. Combine chocolate and butter with pastry well. Pour it in a parchment-lined baking pan and bake in oven for 20-30 minutes until done. Let it rest in the refrigerator for 3 hours then cut into 0.5 inch cubes.

Truffel balls: temper chocholate over a pot of lightly boiling water. Bring cream to a boil then mix with melted chocolate in three portions. Stir until smooth. Pour cream into a 2-inch box lined with plastic foil and put in the refrigerator for a night. Dip a melon baller in hot water and scoop out balls. Dredge balls in crushed almonds.

Orange jelly: soak gelatin leaves in cold water for 10 minutes then squeeze water out. Melt gelatin in the 1/3 orange juice. Warm up the leftover orange juice (do not boil) and mix with gelatin. Pour it into a box lined with plastic foil and put in the refrigerator for 5 hours until set. Cut rounds with a small cutter.

Cocoa tuile: combine all ingredients and spoon pastry in a decorating bag. Push dots into a parchment-lined baking pan (dots shall be 2 inches far from each other at least) and bake in oven at 340°F (180°C) for 12 minutes. Remove from hot baking pan and set aside for 10 minutes.

Passion fruit purée: do the same as you did with orange jelly. Purée set jelly with a blender so as to get a shiny purée.

BALÁZS PETHŐ

CSALOGÁNY26 RESTAURANT

Undoubtedly, one of the current generation's best chefs Balázs Pethő is said to be modest, humble and obsessed. He is passionate about his profession and epitomizes the words 'culinary art'.

'Dreariness is not the strongest side of Hungarian cuisine. The basic techniques, lack of refinement could be used to advantage if chanelled in the right way, mixing the old traditions with the new influences, informing the public taste. I have a curiousity to explore and turn to my feelings and moods for inspiration. I'm determined to push myself to reach my limits. I am a perfectionist and naturally very critical about Csalogány 26. I think Mangalitsa can produce world-class meat if farmed with care and consideration in a controlled way and cooked with the best of techniques.'

PRESSED MANGALITSA NOSE TERRINE WITH HOMEMADE FERMENTED PICKLES

INGREDIENTS (FOR 4 PERSONS):
FOR THE TERRINE:
2 Mangalitsa trotters
15 Mangalitsa noses
8 cups / 2 l water
3 cloves
1/4 star anise
1 bulb garlic
1 white onion, finely chopped
10 black pepper seeds, whole
3.5 oz / 100 g carrot, sliced
2 oz / 50 g parsley root
2 oz / 50 g celery root
2 tbsps / 30 g salt

FOR THE FERMENTED PICKLES:
108 oz / 3 kg pickle, medium sized
8 cups / 2 l water
1/3 cup / 100 g salt
4 cloves of garlic, finely chopped
6 black pepper seeds, whole
4 sprigs dill
3.5 oz / 100 g bread
2 capia sweet peppers

Peel and chop onion, garlic and vegetables. Bring a pot of water to a boil. Put nails, noses into pot with vegetables and spices and simmer until tender. Drain. Place meats into a terrine mold, cover with sieved stock. Press down and put in the refrigerator for at least 2 hours.

Bake capia peppers in hot oven. When cool enough to handle, remove skin and core then dice. Cut the ends of the pickles and stick a knife into them. Place pickles tight into a big jar, layered with spices. Put a slice of bread on the top. Fill the jar with brine of 86°F (30°C) and cover with a kitchen towel. Put jar a warm place (at least 95°F) (95°C). Fermentation will take about 2 days. Remove bread and drain. Mince pickles and mix with baked capia peppers. Serve them as a garnish by the terrine.

RECOMMENDED WINE
GEDEON
Arany Sárfehér (Golden White), 2009

SUMMER BEANS WITH MANGALITSA TROTTERS IN BREADCRUMBS AND MARINATED SQUID

INGREDIENTS (FOR 4 PERSONS):
FOR THE TROTTERS AND SQUID:

6 Mangalitsa trotters
1 bulb garlic
2 bay leaves, whole
6 black pepper seeds, whole
4 squids
1 tbsp olive oil
juice of a lemon segment
juice of 1/2 lime
salt to taste
3.5 oz / 100 g breadcrumbs

FOR THE SUMMER BEANS:

3.5 oz / 100 g string bean
3.5 oz / 100 g wax bean
3.5 oz / 100 g shell bean
4 cloves of garlic, finely chopped
3.5 oz / 100 g celery root
1 tbsp sour cream

Cook trotters and spices in a pressure cooker until tender (about 50 minutes). Remove bones and cool. Dice dredge in breadcrumbs then fry in deep fat.

Clean squids and cut into rings. Sear rings on hot fat then season with olive oil, lime juice, lemon juice and salt.

Peel garlic cloves and cook them in 1 2/3 cups of water with parsley root. Cook beans in salty water without chopping them. Purée the 'soup' of garlic and parsley root in a blender. Combine with beans and thicken with sour cream.

RECOMMENDED WINE
ZARÁNDOK WINE CELLAR
*Misebor Szürkebarát
(Altar wine Pinot gris), 2011*

DONUTS FRIED IN MANGALICA LARD WITH FRUITS, SWEET CORN MOUSSE AND LAVENDER JELLY

INGREDIENTS (FOR 4 PERSONS):
FOR THE DONUTS:

0.4 oz / 10 g yeast
1 2/3 cups / 200 g flour
1/2 cup / 0.1 l milk
1/2 cup / 50 g icing sugar
1.5 tbsps / 20 g butter
2 egg yolks

FOR THE LAVENDER JELLY:

5 cups / 1.2 l lavender-tasted syrup
0.5 oz / 12 g gelatin
1/3 oz / 9 g agar agar
2 tbsps / 10 g icing sugar
1/3 oz / 10 g starch

FOR THE SWEET CORN MOUSSE:

1 ear sweet corn
1/4 cup / 30 g corn flour
1 2/3 cups / 0.4 l milk
1 egg white
1 Vanilla bean

fruits of the season to taste

Combine all ingredients well and knead until smooth. Let it rise for 30 minutes then roll to 0.2-inch thickness. Cut with a cutter (small rounds) and fry in deep Mangalitsa lard at 320°F (160°C).

Bring syrup and agar agar to a boil then add gelatin. Pour into a terrine mold and place it in the refrigerator until solid. Make a mixture of the same quantity of icing sugar and starch. Cut small rectangles from jelly and dredge in this mixture.

Cook corn flour in milk. Cook sweet corn in water. Remove kernels and purée them in a blender with corn flour. Sieve, add egg white and the seeds of Vanilla bean. Pour into a whipping siphon. Serving: Wash fruits well and put them on the bottom of a glass. Press corn mousse on the top and decorate with donuts.

RECOMMENDED WINE
BOTT WINE CELLAR
Tokaji Aszú (6 puttonyos), 2006

ISTVÁN RÁPOLTHY

TUBA TANYA

The farm owner István Rápolthy is the iconic character of Tuba Tanya. He wants to hand on traditions and memories to the new generation through foods, good talks, furniture – and hospitality.

'The oven's heat, the nearness of nature and animals, the season's rotation, the sowing-harvesting and my grandma's recipes are all still present in our everyday life in Tuba Tanya.

A farm must live in harmony with nature. Domestic animals, vegetables and homemade products inspire us during the whole year. That is the tradition and harmony we want to offer to our guests, as simple as our grandparents did.

We couldn't live without domestic animals, they are our ingredients. We have a lot of Mangalitsa scrunching sweet corn or acorn in summer, and as it turns to winter, they give delicate meat to us. Mangalitsa is a very important food, we use every part of it - as our forefathers did. Just some examples: blood with onion, rib soup, roast, feet stew, sausage, ham, bacon, puff pastry, aspic... Some is to be eaten fresh, other must be cured, smoked or marinated. However, don't miss even a tiny bit of it!

SALTY WHITE MANGALITSA BACON
AND HOT PAPRIKA SAUSAGE

INGREDIENTS:
FOR THE SALTY WHITE
MANGALITSA BACON:
White Mangalitsa bacon
(from pig's back – you can leave a thin meat
layer /see photo/)
salt grains

FOR THE HOT PAPRIKA SAUSAGE:
360 oz / 10 kg sausagemeat
(spare rib, shoulder, leg, riblet or bath chap)
7 oz / 200 g red paprika powder, sweet
7 oz / 200 g salt
cca. 1 oz / 15 g red paprika powder, hot
0.5 oz / 5 g black pepper, ground
pinch of white pepper, ground
4 oz / 120 g garlic, crushed
1 tbsp icing sugar

Hungary has a strong tradition of pig slaughtering, and each house has its own secret process or seasoning. It happens in winter – larders got full of sausages, hams and bacons. Lots of delicate things can be made from a Mangalitsa, salty white bacon, brawn, homemade liver paté, bacon with red paprika, sausage, smoked ham, smoked hock, rib of pork or salami for example... The longer time they cure the more delicious their taste will be.

Salty white Mangalitsa bacon
The best salty white bacon is made of Mangalitsa. It has thicker and tastier fat than an 'average' pig so every simple product made of it is a real titbit. Although it is perfect in cooking for replacing lard, the best way to enjoy it is to eat with freshly baked bread and purple onion. It melts in your mouth just like butter...

Scrub bacon with salt and place it into a wooden tub. Layer bacon if you wish but don't forget sprinkle layers with salt. Let it stand for 4 days. Salt absorbed water from bacon during that time. Remove bacon. Clean bacon from salt and layer again, sprinkling every layer with salt. Cover with a cheesecloth and let it cure for a month in a cold place. Remove bacon from tub and clean. Let it cure hung up for an additional 3 weeks.

Hot paprika sausage
Is there anybody who doesn't like homemade paprika sausage? We are not able to produce enough of it, so it is our biggest treasure at the end of summers. Necessary ingredient for many foods, only a small piece is enough to give a smoky feeling to the food. Good food can be prepared only from good ingredients. What is the secret of a good sausage? The proportion of meat and lard, the quality of red paprika and smoking. Our red paprika comes from Kalocsa.

It is highly recommended to mix meats with riblet or bath chap as sausagemeat must contain no less than 20% fat! Cut meats in thin strips and let meatjuice drop out. It takes about 6 hours but it is a very important step, because fresh meat contains a lot of water and if you work with that, your sausage will be wrinkled. Combine meats with spices well and let it stand in a cold place for a night. Ground meats coarsely and stuff into thoroughly cleaned small intestine of pig. Let them dry overnight then smoke over cold beech smoke. Cure them for 6-8 weeks in a cool, airy place.

MANGALITSA FEET STEW

INGREDIENTS (FOR 10 PERSONS):

5 mangalitsa feet
72 oz / 2 kg Mangalitsa shoulder, diced
36 oz / 1 kg onion, finely chopped
10 cloves of garlic, crushed
salt
2 oz / 50 g red paprika powder
black pepper, ground
caraway seed, ground
7 oz / 200 g Mangalitsa lard
3 green peppers, chopped
72 oz / 2 kg potato

Cut feet into pieces and cook in salty water for 1.5 hours. Sauté onion on rendered lard. Add garlic, green pepper and paprika powder. Cover with 2 cups water. When water evaporates add shoulder and feet. Season with black pepper and ground caraway seed. Cover with feet's cooking water and cook until tender. Serve with boiled potato, homemeade bread and pickles.

SAUERKRAUT WITH SMOKED MEAT AND PEARL BARLEY

INGREDIENTS (FOR 10 PERSONS):
FOR THE CHOP:
18 oz / 500 g smoked hock
18 oz / 500 g smoked rib of pork
18 oz / 500 g smoked sausage
18 oz / 500 g pearl barley
54 oz / 1.5 kg sauerkraut (sour cabbage)
7 oz / 200 g onion, finely chopped
5 cloves of garlic, crushed
salt, ground black pepper,
red paprika powder,
4 bay leaves

Heat masonry oven for minimum 1 hour before start baking. Cut hock and rib in bigger pieces and boil them in water with bay leaves for 1 hour. Rinse pearl barley thoroughly in tap water. If sauerkraut is too sour, rinse it in lukewarm water as well. Layer sauerkraut, meats, sausage, pearl barley, onion, garlic and spices in an 8 liter ceramic casserole. Cover with the smoked meats' cooking water. Place casserole in oven and cook it for 1.5-2 hours. Add some cooking water if liquid evaporated. Remove casserole from oven and let it rest for 20 minutes. Serve with sour cream.

LÁSZLÓ RUPRECHT

MANGA RESTAURANT - HERNYÁK ESTATE

Although a consultant of many restaurants, his real favorite is Manga Restaurant in Etyek. He and his friend Tamás Hernyák (see left) run a bistro here in which there two stars: the Mangalitsa and forest mushrooms.

'I really love good markets which I find as inspiring as a beautiful photo of food or a well-compiled menu. You can learn from everyone and everything around you. One of my favorite products and one I'm working closely with at the moment is the Mangalitsa. It is very close to my heart because I can make so many things from it. Presentation is important to me and our guests love the delicate quality of the meat. Hungarian food is not just about using Paprika as is widely thought but we have many fantastic ingredients like Mangalitsa which I hope will take its place internationally.'

MANGALITSA HAM ROLL WITH MOUSSE IN THREE COLORS

INGREDIENTS (FOR 4 PERSONS):
FOR THE GREEN PEA MOUSSE:

6 oz / 160 g green pea
1 spring onion, sliced
2 tbsps honey
1/4 cup / 60 g butter
half bunch of parsley, minced

FOR THE CARROT MOUSSE:

2 bay leaves, whole
1 tbsp brown sugar
7 carrot (200 g)
1/2 tsp cumin

FOR THE POTATO MOUSSE:

4 potatoes, medium, diced
1 bay leaf, whole
3/4 cup / 0.2 l heavy cream
2 tbsps horse radish, grated
1/4 cup / 60 g butter
1 egg yolk
1 tsp Dijon mustard
2/3 cup / 0.15 l grape seed oil
salt and pepper to taste

FOR THE SERVING:

1 apple
12 slices Mangalitsa ham

Sauté green peas with spring onions on honey and butter. Add a small amount of liquid (don't cover vegetables) and simmer until tender. Drain. Put vegetables, 3-4 tbsps cooking liquid and parsley in a blender and purée.

Put bay leaves, a pinch of salt and sugar into a pot of water. Cook the whole carrots in it then purée in a blender with cumin.

Put diced potato, salt, a bay leaf and horse radish in a pot. Cover with cream and cook covered until tender. Remove bay leaf, add butter and purée in a blender.

Mix egg yolk with mustard, flavor with salt and pepper. Carefully add grape seed oil drop by drop and stir constantly until becomes mayonnaise. Add it to potato purée. Fill Mangalitsa ham slices with potato mousse and roll them up.

Serving: Spoon mousses into a decorating bag and make pretty portions on plate. Place ham rolls next to them and garnish with fresh apple, grated horse radish and green peas.

RECOMMENDED WINE
HERNYÁK WINE CELLAR
Zöldveltelini (Green Veltliner), 2011

MANGALITSA CHOP WITH MANGALITSA EAR CONFIT, CELERY ROOT PURÉE AND ROASTED CARROTS

INGREDIENTS (FOR 4 PERSONS):

36 oz / 1 kg Mangalitsa chop with bones in
4 tbsps grape seed oil
1 cup / 250 g butter
1 clove of garlic, finely chopped
3 sprigs fresh rosemary
2 Mangalitsa ears
36 oz / 1 kg Mangalitsa lard
3 bay leaves
3/4 cup / 0.2 l red wine
1 lemon zest
2 cloves of garlic

FOR THE CELERY ROOT PURÉE:

14 oz / 400 g celery root, peeled, diced
6 salvia leaves
2 spring onions, chopped
2/3 cup / 0.15 l white wine
2 eggs
3.5 oz / 100 g breadcrumbs
2/3 cup / 80 g flour

FOR THE ROASTED CARROTS:

4 carrots, small
1 lemon juice
2 tbsps brown sugar
cca. 1/4 cup / 50 g butter
1/4 bunch of fresh coriander
salt and pepper to taste

Sprinkle chop with salt and sear it on the mixture of grape seed oil and butter (butter should be added at the end). Transfer into a baking pan and season with garlic and rosemary then bake in oven at 175°F (80°C) for 2 hours with air circulation. Switch off oven and let meat rest for an additional 20-25 minutes. Do not wash up the pan in which you have seared meat! Cover Mangalitsa ears with rendered lard, add bay leaf, lemon zest, garlic and salt. Confit ears in oven or covered over low heat for 5-6 hours.

Sauté celery dices with salvia leaves and spring onion rings. Flavor with salt and white pepper, cover with white wine. Add vegetable stock or water when wine has evaporated. Simmer celery to doneness. Add liquid constantly when evaporates. Drain (keep the stock). Put celery in a blender with butter and the leftover salvia and purée. Cool and form small balls from pulp. Bread them in flour, egg wash and breadcrumbs and fry in deep hot fat (you can use the melted lard in which ears were confitted).

Peel carrots and cook them in salty water with sugar and lemon juice until tender. Sauté carrots in butter and sprinkle with coriander.

Pour some wine into the pan you have seared the meat in. Add cooking water of the celery and bring to a boil. Drain and thicken with butter. Add butter gradually, dice by dice until thicken. Serving: Cut stripes from ears and bring to a boil together with the gravy.

RECOMMENDED WINE
HERNYÁK WINE CELLAR
Sauvignon Blanc, 2011

MANGALITSA JOWL IN WINE WITH LENTILS AND ROASTED DUCK LIVER

INGREDIENTS (FOR 4 PERSONS):
FOR THE JOWL:
4 Mangalitsa jowls
1/2 cup / 100 g butter
2 tbsps grape seed oil
2 carrots, chopped
1 celery root, small, chopped
1 onion, finely chopped
2 bulbs garlic
3 bay leaves
4 sprigs fresh thyme
1 tbsp tomato purée
3 1/4 cups / 0.8 l red wine

FOR THE LENTILS:
7 oz / 200 g green lentil
3 scallions, finely chopped
3 tbsps / 40 g butter
2 tbsps grape seed oil
2 blanched celery, finely chopped
1 carrot, finely chopped
1 clove of garlic, finely chopped
3/4 cup / 0.2 l red wine
1 bunch of parsley, finely chopped

FOR THE LIVER:
10.5 oz / 300 g fresh spinach leaves
3 cloves of garlic, finely chopped
1/2 cup / 120 g butter
7 oz / 200 g fat duck liver
salt, freshly ground black pepper to taste

Sear jowls on butter then take them out of pan. Pour grape seed oil into the pan and sauté celery root, carrot until brown. Put three cloves of garlic aside. Cut the leftover garlics and onion in half and add to vegetables together with bay leaf and thyme. Add tomato purée. Roast for some minutes then cover with wine. Boil and sprinkle with salt. Place jowls back in pan and simmer covered to doneness. Add some water or vegetable stock if needed. Remove meat from gravy. Drain dripping (don't sieve) on it.

Soak lentils in cold water for 2-3 hours. Sauté scallions on the mixture of butter and grape seed oil. Add blanched celery, carrot, garlic, parsley and lentils. Cover with red wine. Flavor with salt and simmer covered to doneness. There shouldn't be too much water on lentils - you'd rather add water spoon by spoon if needed.

Wash spinach leaves and toss with a mixture of butter and garlic. Purée in a blender.

Remove veins from liver (it is more comfortable to work with a liver of room temperature) and cut into slices. Put in the refrigerator for 30 minutes. Sprinkle with salt and pepper and grill in a hot nonstick pan on all sides. Serving: Place liver slices on a plate with spinach, lentils and jowls.

RECOMMENDED WINE
HERNYÁK WINE CELLAR
Pinot Noir, 2011

ÁKOS SÁRKÖZI

WINEKITCHEN

Although he doesn't do anything special, just cooks 'simple, tasty foods', Ákos Sárközi is one of the biggest promises for Hungarian culinary art. His humility, professionalism and gastronomical sense of humor have won him many awards, including his black sour cream made Winekitchen.

'There are no gastronomic principles for me - my dishes are determined by flavors and shapes. I prefer simple, tasty food and I give as much attention to shapes as to colors – sometimes they are my starting points during cooking. I am Hungarian so my motivations are the flavors from my home. My first experiences of cooking were gained in the family kitchen at home and have had a big impact on me and those memories continue in every dish I make. Personal relationships with the suppliers of produce is very important to me and I continue to source the best ingredients. Mangalitsa means Hungary for me. I regularly work with it and use every single part of it. I hope this high quality product will become widely available soon and becomes the success story of our country – no more goose liver, please!'

167

MANGALITSA BONBON WITH CAULIFLOWER AND GREEN APPLE

INGREDIENTS (FOR 4 PERSONS):
FOR THE BONBON:
18 oz / 500 g Mangalitsa chuck
2 carrots, sliced
3 shallots, sliced
1 clove of garlic, sliced
1 bunch of blanched celery, sliced
1 bunch of fresh thyme
1 bunch of fresh rosemary
18 oz / 500 g Mangalitsa lard
1 bunch of chive
1 tbsp pine nut
half bunch of parsley
3/4 cup / 0.2 l beetroot juice
0.5 oz / 15 g gelantin
salt, freshly ground black pepper

FOR THE CAULIFLOWER:
1 cauliflower, medium
1 bunch of saffron
1 tbsp cheese spread
1/2 cup / 100 g butter, soft
salt
ground white pepper
sugar to taste

FOR THE GREEN APPLE:
2 green apples
2 tbsps balsamic vinegar
6 tbsps olive oil

Sprinkle chuck with salt and pepper and place into a baking pan with thick wall. Put sliced carrots, onions, shallots, garlic and celery around meat. Season with rosemary and thyme and pour rendered lard on it. Cover with aluminium foil and bake in oven at 265°F (130°C) for 2-3 hours. Cool in pan. Remove from lard and cut into small dices. Roast pine nuts in a nonstick pan and blend with meat and freshly chopped hive. Flavor with parsley and pepper. Add some of the leftover lard to make it juicy. Put in the refrigerator for an hour then form balls with wet hand. Bring beetroot juice to a boil with soaked gelatin. Dip meat balls into it. Repeat twice dipping if needed. Keep bonbons in refrigerator until serving. If you use vegetable gelatin you can serve balls warm as well.

Break cauliflowers' florets off (put 4 florets apart). Steam them in water with salt and sugar. Drain and purée in a blender together with butter and cheese spread. Flavor with salt and ground white pepper to taste - your gravy is done. Cover the 4 cauliflower florets and saffron with 4 cups water. Add salt and sugar to the water and blanch florets (they must remain crunchy). Drain and cool. Warm up in butter before serving.

Serving: Cut green apples in small dices and blend well with olive oil and chive. Place a meat ball on a plate and decorate with florets, gravy and apple dices.

RECOMMENDED WINE
TAMÁS SZENT
Furmint, 2011

MANGALITSA TONGUE LASAGNE WITH BLACK SOUR CREAM AND ZUCCHINI

INGREDIENTS (FOR 4 PERSONS):
FOR THE LASAGNE:

4 Mangalitsa tongues
2 bay leaves, whole
1 clove of garlic
10 black pepper seeds, whole
1 leek
2 shallots
2 sprigs thyme
2 sprigs rosemary
7 oz / 200 g chicken breast
1/2 cup / 0.1 l heavy cream

FOR THE BLACK SOUR CREAM:

2 cups / 0.5 l sour cream
3.5 oz / 100 g cheese spread
3 gelatin leaves
1/2 cup / 0.1 l heavy cream
1 tbsp / 2 g salt
1 oz / 20 g cuttlefish ink

FOR THE WHITE SOUR CREAM:

2 cups / 0.5 l sour cream
3.5 oz / 100 g cheese spread
3 gelatin leaves
1/2 cup / 0.1 l heavy cream
1 tbsp / 2 g salt

FOR THE ZUCCHINI:

10.5 oz zucchini
1/4 cup olive oil
green pepper

RECOMMENDED WINE
KISLAKI WINE MANUFACTURE
Pinot Noir, 2011

Place all ingredients into a large pot, except chicken breast and cream. Cover with water and simmer until tender. Peel off tongues' skin when still warm. Place tongue back to pot and let cool in its cooking water. Cut chicken breast into small pieces then purée in a blender with cream. Sprinkle with salt, pepper and sieve. Take two baking pans of terrine molds of the same size. Line one mold with plastic foil. Foil must be longer and wider than the mold. Cut cool tongues into thin slices and place them tightly on the bottom of the mold. Spread with chicken cream. Repeat layering until running out of ingredients. Cover with foil and press down with the other pan/mold. If you have a steamer, steam it at 195°F (90°C) for 20 minutes. If you don't have: bake it in oven at 175°F (80°C) for 25 minutes with air circulation. When done, cool and put in the refrigerator (still pressed down). Cut only when it is cold. Sear on all sides before serving.

Blend all ingredients but gelatin and heat to 120°F (50°C). Soak gelatin leaves in water for 5 minutes. Squeeze them and add to the mixture. Spoon into a plastic box lined with foil and put in the refrigerator. Dice when cool. Prepare the white sour cream the same way. Serving: Place sour cream dices on the top of lasagne with a chess pattern.

Cut zucchini into thin slices. Fry them on shallow fat and sprinkle with salt and green pepper.

CURD CHEESE PIE WITH RASPBERRY

INGREDIENTS (FOR 4 PERSONS):
FOR THE CURD CHEESE FILLING:
18 oz / 500 g fresh curd cheese
7 oz / 200 g soft cheese spread
1 cup / 100 g icing sugar
1 lime, zest and juice
3/4 cup / 0.2 l heavy cream
4 gelatin leaves

FOR THE PASTRY:
5.5 oz / 150 g butter cookie
1/2 cup / 125 g butter
1/3 cup / 40 g icing sugar

FOR THE SORBET:
flesh of 36 oz / 1 kg fresh mango
2 oz / 50 g honey or glucose
1/2 cup / 0.1 l water
1 cup / 200 g sugar

FOR THE PINK PEPPERCORN CRUMBS:
1 cup / 250 g butter
2 cups / 250 g flour
2 1/4 cups / 250 g sugar
1 1/2 cups / 150 g almond, sliced
1 tbsp pink peppercorn

FOR THE DECORATION:
3.5 oz / 100 g fresh raspberry

Preheat oven to 355°F (108°C). Flake cookies and mix with butter and icing sugar. Pat pastry into an oiled and floured baking pan and put in the refrigerator for 10 minutes. Bake in oven for 6-7 minutes with air circulation. Cool.

Soak gelatin leaves in cold water. Blend curd cheese, cheese spread with icing sugar, lime juice and lime zest well. Whip cream until it forms soft peaks and add to the curd cheese carefully. Heat 2 tbsps water in a pan and melt gelatin leaves. Cool to room-temperature and add to curd cheese, stirring constantly. Spoon curd cheese onto the pastry and put in the refrigerator until set. Place raspberries on the top.

Boil water, glucose or honey with sugar. Simmer for 2 minutes. Put mango flesh in a blender with syrup, purée and sieve. Put it into the deep-freeze and beat it with a whisk in every 15 minutes until it can be formed with a spoon. May be made in an ice cream maker as well.

Preheat oven to 355°F (180°C). Combine all ingredients and grate into a baking pan. Bake in oven for 3-4 minutes with air circulation until golden brown.

Serving: Place a slice of pie on a plate, garnish with sorbet and crumbs. Decorate plate with fruit-purée dots.

RECOMMENDED WINE
TOKAJ OREMUS
Late Harvest

KONRÁD SCHIESZL

SCHIESZL RESTAURANT

As you take a look at the indicated founding year you can see the Schieszl family has been working in hospitality for more than a century. The restaurant and the wine house locate in the main street of Budakalász. The latter is led by Konrád Schieszl senior, the former is ruled by his son. The two types of hospitality, restaurant and wine house are stick together like father and son. In Schieszl, everything is balanced, we can feel the tranquility in the first moment after entering.

'I find it important to offer new tastes to my guests or to offer traditional foods in modern way. Our cuisine is based on classical Hungarian gastronomy. We use only fresh, local ingredients, mostly kraut or old Hungarian food just as seasonal favorites like trout and zander.

Our guests can have homemade products, fruit juices, jams, cheeses, Mangalitsa hams and pestos. These titbits can be taken home together with the wines and pálinkas of our Wine House. As a matter of fact I have to say that loving good wine is a tradition in our family. The Schieszl family works in an area of 10 acres, redeemed and recultivated after World War II. We produce our wines made of grapes from other territories (Balaton Uplands, Gyöngyöstarján, Villány) also in that modern Winery in order to offer as good wine to our guests as our foods are!'

MANGALITSA HAM

INGREDIENTS:
hind legs of Mangalitsa sow,
9 000-10 800 oz / 250-300 kg each

Trim hind legs, create a nice shape and scrub with salt grains thoroughly.

Let it be cured for 4-5 weeks. Turn round every single day, adding salt continously.

Cover with water and let it be cured for an additional 3-4 weeks. Turn round every day.

Remove from salty water and rinse in lukewarm water.

Soak in icecold water for twice 24 hours then pat dry.

Smoke for a week, this means: smoke every second days and have a day break between.

Place into a curing chamber after smoking.

RECOMMENDED WINE
SCHIESZL WINE HOUSE
Blaufränkisch, 2012

MANGALITSA HEART SOUP

INGREDIENTS (FOR 4 PERSONS):

14 oz / 200 g Mangalitsa heart
4-5 medium carrots, chopped
4-5 medium parsley roots, chopped
1 fresh celery root, chopped
2 onions
1 bulb garlic
5-6 spring onions, chopped
2/3 cup / 0.2 l sour cream
3.5 oz / 100 g zucchini, chopped
3 tbsps / 40 g Mangalitsa lard
fresh parsley
lemon
salt
ground black pepper
bay leaves to taste

Wash heart thoroughly and place into a pot of water. Add 4 cloves of garlic, 1 whole onion, 1 bay leaf and salt. Bring to a boil, reduce heat and simmer for 2 hours.

Chop the other onion and gently sauté it on rendered lard. Add carrots, parsley roots and celery roots, sauté them then cover with stock. Cook for 25-30 minutes. Remove vegetables for decoration. Purée the leftover in blender thoroughly, add sour cream and bring to a boil. Add zucchini, spring onions, the cooked vegetables and sliced heart. Bring to a boil once more and flavor with salt and lemon juice. Serve with parsley.

TIP: Add some white wine to the stock or serve with whole-grain mustard and horse radish so as to be more piquant.

RECOMMENDED WINE
SCHIESZL WINE HOUSE
Welschriesling, 2013

MANGALITSA CHUCK WITH ROASTED EAR AND SPICY STEWED PLUM

INGREDIENTS (FOR 4 PERSONS):
FOR THE SPARE RIB:
36 oz / 1 kg Mangalitsa chuck
7 oz / 200 g Mangalitsa ear
1 bay leaf, whole
4 bulbs of garlic
2 onions
1 bell pepper
1 tomato
salt
ground black pepper
1.5 oz / 40 g Mangalitsa lard

FOR THE STEWED PLUM:
14 oz / 400 g plum
1 star anise
1 bay leaf, whole
honey
horse radish
apple balsam of Tokaj (special balsamic vinegar with apple cider vinegar and must) to taste

Put ears in a pot, cover with water, add 4 cloves of garlic, 1 whole onion, bay leaf and salt. Bring to a boil, reduce heat and simmer for 2 hours. Remove the meat and pat dry. Fry sliced chuck on rendered lard for short time then remove from pan. Cut onion into two halves and put them in lard with the leftover garlic cloves. Sauté them, place meat back to the pan with salt and ground pepper. Cover with some stock (Meat must be fried rather then cooked) and simmer. Add bell pepper and tomato.

Bring 7 oz water to a boil. Add star anise, bay leaf, 2-3 slices of horse radish and cook for 10 minutes. Add pitted plums and add 2 tbsps honey and bring to a boil once more. Remove from heat and add Apple Balsam to taste. Serve in small jars.

Place ears in a nonstick pan and broil under a brick. Remove garlic from pan and purée in a blender.

Serving: Place chuck and ears on a plate. Garnish with garlic purée and stewed plums in jars.

TIP: Stewed plums may be flavored with a small amount of chili. May be served with freshly baked homemade bread.

RECOMMENDED WINE
SCHIESZL WINE HOUSE
Cserszegi Fűszeres, 2013

ZOLTÁN SOVÁK

WALTER RESTAURANT

Although Perbál is a small town with about 2000 inhabitants, there is a real gastronomic revolution there. The leading figures are Zoltán Sovák and László Ruprecht, creative chefs of Walter Restaurant. They wanted to establish an old-fashioned inn with simple, tasty foods, local commodities, Hungarian flavors – and love.

'Hungarian cuisine is defined by its seduction of foreigners with its flavors, simplicity and honesty. Some Hungarian dishes can appear to be stodgey but can be prepared in a healthier way while still retaining the flavors. Since we are a traditional, rural restaurant, we work with Hungarian produce. Our menu shows how much we love working with Mangalitsa meat. We love each part for different reasons, roasted or grilled tenderloin, clerk's steak with spices and Mangalitsa jowl stewed or steamed in red wine. I am glad that Mangalitsa is enjoying a renaissance and hope that it will be enjoyed both by Hungarians and foreigners alike.'

MANGALITSA PÂTÉ IN TWO STYLES

INGREDIENTS (FOR 4 PERSONS):
FOR THE PÂTÉ:
7 oz / 200 g smoked Mangalitsa tongue
9 oz / 250 g Mangalitsa hock, boneless
7 oz / 200 g Mangalitsa shoulder
9 oz / 250 g Mangalitsa heart
15 black pepper seeds, whole
6 bay leaves, whole
3 sprigs rosemary
3 onions, small, quartered
7 cloves of garlic
1 bunch of parsley, finely chopped

FOR THE BREADING:
1 egg
1/3 cup / 50 g flour
5.5 oz / 150 g breadcrumbs
2 tbsps sunflower oil

FOR THE PARSLEY GRAVY:
5.5 oz / 150 g parsley root
2 bunches of parsley

FOR THE SWEET CORN MOUSSE:
3 ears of corn
1/4 cup / 50 g butter
3.5 oz / 100 g horse radish, grated

Cook tongues, hearts and hock in separate pots of salty water. Mind the quantity of salt, tongues can be salty originally! Place 1-1 sprigs rosemary, 2-2 bay leaves 1-1 onion, 2-2 cloves of garlic and 5-5 black pepper seeds in each pot. Simmer them for 3-4 hours until tender. Remove meats from cooking water and let cool. Trim skin from tongue and cut meat into small cubes. Dice hock and hearts as well. Mince Mangalitsa shoulder. Flavor with salt, black pepper, a minced clove of garlic and parsley. Combine well. Add meats. Spoon in a rectangular baking pan and press down. Bake in oven at 210°F (100°C) for 40 minutes. Cool when done then put in the refrigerator for 2-3 hours, still pressed down.

Bring 1 1/4 cups cold water to a boil with peeled parsley roots and a pinch of salt. Boil it for 30 minutes, reduce by one third. Remove roots and chop parsley leaves into the cooking water. Boil once (do not cook for long time in order to keep its color). Purée in a blender.

Cut off kernels from ears and sauté them on butter. Add horse radish. Sprinkle with salt and steam until tender. Purée in a blender when still warm.

Cut cold pâté into 8 pieces. Dredge 4 pieces in egg wash and crumbs. Repeat process twice. Pan-fry them for a short time until golden, then bake them in oven at 355°F (180°C) for 8 minutes to doneness.

Serving: Place a fried and a cold slice of pâté on each plate and garnish with sweet corn mousse and parsley gravy.

RECOMMENDED WINE
BUSSAY WINE CELLAR
Csörnyeföldi Rajnai Rizling (Riesling)

CLERK'S STEAK IN OAT FLOUR WITH PORCINI AND KOHLRABI DUET

INGREDIENTS (FOR 4 PERSONS):
FOR THE STEAK:
29 oz / 800 g Clerk's steak
43 oz / 1.2 kg Mangalitsa lard
1 onion, finely chopped
4 cloves of garlic, finely chopped
3 bay leaves
8 black pepper seeds, whole
1 sprig rosemary
1 cup / 150 g oat flour
2 eggs
2 cups / 0.5 l olive oil

FOR THE KOHLRABI DUET:
14 oz / 400 g kohlrabi
2 tbsps / 50 g salt
1/2 cup / 120 g butter
7 oz / 200 g porcini

RECOMMENDED WINE
**ST ANDREA WINERY
AND WINE CELLAR**
Kovászó Chardonnay

Sprinke steak slices with salt and set aside for a while. Render lard in a large pot and put steak slices, onion pieces, garlics, bay leaves, pepper seeds and rosemary in. Confit it in oven at 195°F (90°C) for 3-4 hours until tender. When done, transfer meat into a terrine mold and press down. Don't squeeze lard out. Put in the refrigerator for 2-3 hours.

Peel kohlrabi and cut into 8, 1.2x1.5-inch sized rectangulars. Blanch them in salty water. Cut the leftover kohlrabi into cubes and steam in the half butter, adding some cooking water to it. Flavor with salt and pepper. Purée in a blender.

Take cold meat out of the terrine mold and cut into 8 slices. Dredge in oat flour and egg wash. Repeat process and fry it in deep fat. Pat dry.

Cut porcini into cubes. Sauté on the half of the leftover butter and sprinkle with salt. Serving: Sauté kohlrabi rectangulars on butter and serve together with kohlrabi mousse and breaded clerk's steak. Garnish with porcini.

TENDERLOIN WITH BEETROOT AND BARLEY RISOTTO WITH GREEN PEAS

INGREDIENTS (FOR 4 PERSONS):
FOR THE TENDERLOIN:

29 oz / 800 g Mangalitsa tenderloin
1 sprig rosemary, finely chopped
1/2 cup / 0.1 l oil
3 tbsps / 60 g salt
1/2 tsp black pepper, ground

FOR THE BEETROOT:

7 oz / 200 g beetroot
2 tbsps sunflower oil
1/4 cup / 50 g butter
salt to taste

FOR THE RISOTTO:

12 oz / 350 g green pea in pod
cca. 1/4 cup / 50 g butter
4-5 cups / 1.2 l broth or vegetable stock
7 oz / 200 g barley, hulled
1 onion, small, minced
1/2 cup / 0.1 l white wine
1 bunch of parsley, finely chopped

Preheat oven to 300°F (150°C). Wash beetroot thoroughly. Pour oil on them, sprinkle with salt. Bake in oven for about 3 hours until tender. Baking time depends on the size of beetroots. Cool, peel and dice. Sauté on butter. Flavor with salt.

Shell peas then steam them on butter until tender with broth or vegetable stock. Purée in a blender. Wash barley in cold water and dry. Sauté onion on butter then add barley. When barley is hot, pour white wine onto the walls of the pan (do not pour directly onto the barley). Add pea purée and simmer, stirring constantly for 20 minutes to doneness. Add parsley at the end.

Preheat oven to 355°F. (180°C) Trim membranes and upper part from meat. Scrub with pepper and salt, sprinkle with rosemary. Sear in a pan on all sides then bake in oven for 6-8 minutes with air circulation. It should remain pink in the center. Cut into 4 pieces and serve with risotto and beetroot.

RECOMMENDED WINE
JÁSDI WINE CELLAR
Siralomvágó Olaszrizling

ATTILA TATÁR

LOTUS THERME HOTEL

The regulars of Lotus Therme Hotel & Spa**** – and there are a lot of them – expect to be served with new and up-to-date dishes from time to time. Answering that demand we change our menu more times a year, with a special focus on seasonal ingredients.

'Our guests look for traditional, Hungarian tastes but they are open to something new as well. As for myself, I love working with Hungarian ingredients, and I work only with the best of them. Manglitsa is the perfect choice for me because I can't imagine meat more Hungarian than that perfect quality pork. Its taste is suitable for traditional foods, but good for discovering new things too. A perfect meat for everybody who loves cooking. But of course, a good meat is not enough for good food!

I don't think that the quality of a cuisine could be a question of luck. There is extremely hard work and creativity behind. My biggest challenge is not to cook what our guest whishes but to find out what it is!'

LUNG SOUP WITH SOUR CREAM
AND POTATO DUMPLINGS

INGREDIENTS (FOR 4 PERSONS):
FOR THE SOUP:

18 oz / 500 g Mangalitsa lung
1 small onion, whole
2-3 cloves of garlic, whole
1 bay leaf, whole
5 black pepper seeds, whole
2 tbsps Mangalitsa lard
2 tbsps flour
1 carrot, medium
1 celery root, medium
celery stalk
2/3 cup / 0.2 l sour cream
lemon
sugar
salt

FOR THE POTATO DUMPLINGS:

1 potato, large
1 egg
1 onion, small, minced
1.5 oz / 50 g smoked bacon, chopped
2 tbsps flour
salt
ground nutmeg
ground black pepper

Trim fat, vein and membranes from lung and place into a pot of water. Add bay leaf, garlic, onion and bring to simmer until tender. When cool enough to handle cut into 0.6x0.6-inch cubes. Sauté minced onion on lard, sprinkle with sugar and pour lung's cooking water into it. Dice and add peeled vegetables. Add lung when vegetables are half done. Cook until tender then thicken with a mixture of flour and sour cream. Flavor with lemon juice and freshly minced celery stalk. Serve with separately cooked potato dumplings.

Peel potatoes and cook them until tender. Drain and mash when cool enough to handle. Render minced bacon and sauté the finely chopped onion on lard. Combine all ingredients. Add 1 tbsp sour cream if too tough. Form pastry into small lumps with wet hands and cook them in salty water.

RECOMMENDED WINE
LAPOSA
4 Hegy Olaszrizling, 2013

MANGALITSA ROAST
WITH BACON STEW AND DÖDÖLLE
(HUNGARIAN POTATO DUMPLINGS)

INGREDIENTS (FOR 4 PERSONS):

28 oz / 800 g Mangalitsa chuck
salt, ground black pepper
marjoram
garlic, crushed
1 small onion, minced
7 oz / 200 g smoked bacon, diced
3.5 oz / 100 g pearl onion
1tbsp red paprika powder
3.5 oz / 10 g bell pepper, diced

FOR THE DUMPLINGS:

42.5 oz potato
2 2/3 cups flour
Mangalitsa lard
salt

Trim fat and tendon from chuck then cut into large pieces. Place meat to a pot with lard. Sprinkle with onion, salt, ground pepper and marjoram. Add a small amount of water and simmer covered until tender, then sauté uncovered. Flavor with freshly crushed garlic. Render bacon. Put pearl onion on melted lard and sauté. Add bell pepper dices and red pepper. Pour a small amount of water or broth and cook until thicken.

Peel potatoes and slice. Put them in a pot and cover with water. Bring to a boil and cook until tender. Drain and mash with flour. Cut small lumps from pastry with a spoon and fry them in lard.

Serve with tomato salad, sour cream and purple onion.

RECOMMENDED WINE
KONYÁRI
Shyraz, 2011

WHITE HONEY CAKE
WITH LAVENDER-VANILLA ICE CREAM

INGREDIENTS (FOR 4 PERSONS):
FOR THE CAKE:
1 egg
1.5 oz / 40 g Mangalitsa lard
1 tsp baking soda
2 tbsps honey
3 tbsps milk
3/4 cup / 150 g sugar
3 cups / 450 g flour

FOR THE FILLING:
2 cups / 0.5 l milk
5 tbsps semolina
2/3 cup / 150 g butter
1 1/4 cups / 230 g sugar
1 lemon, zest

FOR THE ICE CREAM:
1 cup / 0.25 l milk
1 cup / 0.25 l heavy cream
4 egg yolks
1/2 cup / 100 g sugar
3.5 oz / 100 g mascarpone
lavender flower

Combine all ingredients except flour in a pot over medium heat until smooth then add flour. Knead on a lightly floured surface and form pastry into 4 smooth balls with your hands. Set aside for 30 minutes. Roll to thin and bake them separately on oiled, floured baking pan.

Preparation of the filling: Bring milk to a boil then add semolina. Reduce heat and simmer until semolina get thick and tender. Remove from flame. Stir sugar with butter and add to semolina when it is cool enough to handle. Flavor with lemon zest. Layer cakes with filling let rest for a day. Pour melted white chocolate on top.

Serve with lavender-vanilla ice cream.

Bring milk and cream to a boil and add lavender flowers. Beat egg yolks and sugar then add mascarpone. Combine the two mixtures over medium flame, stirring constantly and clot. Cool. Place in the freezer. Stir from time to time until creamy.

RECOMMENDED WINE
**PINOT GRIS
FROM LESENCETOMAJ**
Late Harvest, 2009

LAJOS TAKÁCS

LACIPECSENYE

The Lacipecsenye may be young but already a legend. Its motto is: We were born to enjoy small things. Small things, such as childhood summers in Káli Basin with their memories and special scents which have been inspiring Lajos Takács. Or such as liver with Sichuan pepper and lavender honey. That was inspired by the Mangalitsa.

'My guiding principles are artfulness, commitment and honesty. We use fresh ingredients, sourced locally and bought fresh daily. Our menu is created daily so there is no pressure to buy anything that isn't in season. I find this motivating and inspirational. My grandpa's liberalism and my grandma's kindness were determining factors in my childhood. I love Mangalitsa very much because of it taste and consistency and wish it every success in the future.'

STUFFED BELL PEPPER WITH EXTRAS

INGREDIENTS (FOR 4 PERSONS):
FOR THE STUFFED BELL PEPPER:
2-3 green, yellow and red bell peppers
1/4 oz / 7.5 g vegetable gelantin
1/4 cup / 50 ml sherry vinegar
1/4 cup / 50 ml champagne vinegar

FOR THE STUFFING:
10.5 oz / 300 g hock, diced
1 onion, finely chopped
1 clove of garlic
2 sprigs thyme
2 parsley roots
1 bay leaf
1/2 cup / 0.1 l white wine
1 tbsp Mangalitsa lard
2-3 button mushrooms, brown, finely chopped
7 oz / 200 g sausages for roasting, Italian style
10.5 oz / 300 g Mangalitsa jowl (cca. 2 pieces)
2 cloves of garlic 2 sprigs thyme
1 oz / 30 g Mangalitsa lard

FOR THE EXTRAS:
peeled ginger root, size of a finger
cca. 1 cup / 0.2-0.3 l oil
(grape seed oil, sesame oil, peanut oil)
2 cloves of garlic
2 chili peppers
1 tbsp vinegar
1 tbsp furikake (Japanese spice mix)
4 sunflower sprout

RECOMMENDED WINE
TAMÁS SZENT
Kishegy (Handmade Champagne), 2009

Remove skin, core and seeds of bell peppers. Purée them in a blender (different colors shall be separated) and sieve. Flavor with salt and pepper. Add champagne vinegar to the yellow and the green juice and sherry vinegar to the red juice. Bring them to a boil (still separately) with warm gelatin powder and pour onto a plastic tray. Cool. Cut them into 6-inch squares.

Make a traditional stew from the diced hock but do not add red paprika powder. When almost done, add chopped mushroom and cook to doneness. This is for the green bell pepper jelly.

Crack garlic with its skin on then sautée it with the thyme on rendered lard. Add Mangalitsa jowl and sear. Transfer jowls, garlic and thyme into a bigger pan. Flavor with salt and pepper, cover with lard. Confit covered for 1.5-2 hours in oven or over low heat. The temperature of the lard shouldn't exceed 212°F (100°C). Cool. Remove meat from lard. Separate lard and dripping. Pull apart meat fibres with a fork and pour drained dripping on it. This is for the yellow bell pepper jelly.

Pan-broil sausages then chop finely. This is for the red bell pepper jelly.

Spoon stuffings into the centers of the squares and fold them (see photo).

Serving: Cut ginger root into Julienne and fry them in deep fat. Place it on the green jelly. Cut thin slices from garlic and chili. Toss them with vinegar. Place it on the yellow jelly. Sprinkle red jelly with sunflower sprout and furikake.

MANGALITSA LIVER WITH LAVENDER HONEY, SICHUAN PEPPER AND WILD STRAWBERRY

INGREDIENTS (FOR 4 PERSONS):
FOR THE LIVER:
14 oz / 400 g Mangalitsa liver
2 oz / 50 g Mangalitsa lard
16 salvia leaves
3.5 oz / 100 g lavender honey (or 3.5 oz / 100 g locust honey and 1 tbsp lavender)
1.5 oz / 40 g sherry vinegar
cca. 1 cup / 0.2-0.3 l oil (grape seed, sesame or peanut oil)
freshly ground Sichuan pepper
Maldon salt to taste
12 wild strawberries

Trim membranes, veins from liver and cut into half-inch slices. Sear them on all sides on Mangalitsa lard. Let them rest on a grate. Fry salvia leaves in deep fat then pat dry.

Heat and mix lavender honey with vinegar. If you don't have lavender honey, place lavender into locust honey and heat for 30 minutes at 175°F (80°C).

Serving: Sear liver slices again and pat dry. Cut them into three and place to a plate. Pour honey around them and place salvia leaves on the top. Sprinkle with Maldon salt. Garnish with strawberries and freshly ground Sichuan pepper.

RECOMMENDED WINE
BUSSAY WINE CELLAR
Csörnyeföldi Tramini, 2009

JAPANESE PORK WITH GOBO

INGREDIENTS (FOR 4 PERSONS):
29 oz / 800 g Mangalitsa bacon (boneless)
1/2 cup / 0.1 l sake
1/2 cup / 0.1 l mirin
1/2 cup / 0.1 l dry Szamorodni (special white wine from Tokaj)
1/2 cup / 0.1 sweet Szamorodni (special white wine from Tokaj)
1/2 cup / 0.1 l Japanese soy sauce
1 cup / 0.2 l dashi
1/2 cup / 0.1 chicken stock
1/3 cup / 50 g flour
grape seed, sesame or peanut oil for pre-frying
10.5 oz / 300 g gobo (beggar's buttons)
7 oz / 200 g broad bean, parboiled (can be replaced with string bean or green soy bean)
salt
freshly ground black pepper to taste

FOR THE DECORATION:
string bean strout
black sea salt flakes

Cut meat into 4 pieces. Flavor with salt and pepper. Dredge in flour and pre-fry them on very shallow fat. Place them in a big pan and cover with all liquid ingredients. Simmer for 2 hours over low heat until tender. Add peeled gobo before done. When done, remove meat and gobo. Transfer them in a plate and cover with plastic foil or wet kitchen towel. Skim fat from cooking water and reduce by third. Put gobo into a pan and spoon 3-4 tbsps reduced cooking water on it. Stir and fry until gobo is coated. Pour reduced gravy on meat and place into the oven (grill mode). Place meat on the lowest grate. Heat must come from above. The gravy will be caramelized. Cut meats into halves and chop gobo. Place them on a plate and spread with broad bean. Pour the leftover gravy and garnish with string bean strouts and black sea salt flakes.

RECOMMENDED WINE
TIBOR GÁL
Pinot Noir, 2008

PÉTER VÁRVIZI

ASTORIA – MIRROR CAFÉ

Despite the fact that Péter Várvízi is a leading figure of his cookery generation, he is extremely humble and determined. He spends time every year working and learning in some of the world's best restaurants. He is very precise and exact in measurments in his recipes. This precision might explain the the strange habit that he wears two watches, one on each arm!

'Science and art are side by side in 21st century cuisine. The more success we have in harmonizing them, the more interesting the dishes will be. However, we have to accept that the more rational the world is, the more we need art and individualism. A good dish can be interesting for me when there is hard, complex work in the background, carried out by precise technologies. Despite that complexity, the result should be understood by the consumer and flavors offer surprises and games. Red Paprika doesn't just make Hungarian cuisine and it's difficult to get rid of that stereotype. For us to proceed forward we need to know the culture, natural and geographical values of the Carpathian Basin. In my recipes, I use sugar beet, scallions, celery and rue because they are Hungarian, just like Mangalitsa. It gives excellent meat if well treated during breeding, feeding, slaughtering and production. It is a popular Hungarian commodity which needs to be respected.'

NORWAY POUT FILLET
WITH MANGALITSA HAM AND SPINACH

INGREDIENTS (FOR 4 PERSONS):
FOR THE FILLET:
11 oz / 320 g Norway pout
1/4 cup / 40 g olive oil
1 sprig French tarragon
sea salt grains

FOR THE SPINACH:
10.5 oz / 300 g spinach
2 cloves of garlic, sliced
1/4 cup / 50 g heavy cream
1 tbsp / 10 g butter
1/2 cup / 20 g water
8 baby carrots
7 oz / 200 g pearl onion
14 oz / 400 g eggplant
1 1/4 cups / 0.3 l olive oil
4 slices of Mangalitsa ham
1 radish
2 curly-leaved parsley
1 oz / 20 g fresh spinach
salt
black pepper to taste

Sprinkle fish with salt. Let it rest for 15 minutes then wash in cold water and pat dry. Cut into four slices and place them in the refrigerator for at least 3 hours. Sprinkle with salt again. Place 3-3 tarragon leaves on the skinny side of the fillets. Roast them in a nonstick pan, skinny side shall be below. Don't turn slices!

Preheat oven to 375°F (190°C). Steam carrots. Cut eggplant in half. Brush with olive oil, flavor with salt and bake in oven. Cool.

Wash spinach leaves thoroughly and cut off stems. Heat a pan, pour water in then add butter, garlic and spinach. Flavor with salt and pepper. Steam for some minutes then transfer to the serving plate.

Pour cream in the same pan, add pearl onion and reduce. Pour gravy around the spinach. Place fish fillets on spinach (skinny side up) and Mangalitsa ham slices on the top. Garnish with steamed carrots and eggplant. Decorate with curly-leaved parsley and fresh spinach.

RECOMMENDED WINE
ENDRE SZÁSZI
Badacsonyi Kéknyelű, 2011

MANGALITSA CHOP WITH SMOKED BREAD GRAVY AND SUGAR BEET LEAVES

INGREDIENTS (FOR 4 PERSONS):

FOR THE CHOP:
14 oz / 400 g Mangalitsa chop
1 sprig thyme
2 tbsps sunflower oil
1.5 tbsps / 20 g butter

FOR THE GARNISH:
10.5 oz / 300 g sugar beet leaf
1 clove of garlic
2 tbsps / 15-20 g butter

FOR THE SCALLION:
8 scallions
1 tbsp / 10 g sugar
1/4 cup / 50 g butter

FOR THE FLOWER SALAD:
2 fresh celery roots
2 tbsps olive oil
2 sprigs rue
3 sprigs broad bean flower
0.5 oz / 10 g wild sorrel
pinch of salt flake (2 g)
1 lemon zest
1 purple onion

FOR THE BREAD GRAVY:
1 egg
2 oz / 50 g smoked, toasted bread
1/2 cup / 125 ml sunflower oil

Heat sunflower oil and butter. Sprinkle chop with salt, pepper and thyme. Fry on all sides.

Wash sugar beet leaves thoroughly (use only young ones). Melt butter in a pan, add a tbsp water then sugar beet leaves. Steam for 10-20 seconds. Flavor with salt and pepper.

Put scallions in a pot and cover with water. Add salt, sugar and bring to a boil. Reduce until water evaporates and sugar and onion is caramelized.

Cut celery into thin slices. Mix with other ingredients and place on the meat.

Boil egg for 6 minutes. Peel and purée in a blender with a small amount of water. Add grinded smoked, toasted bread then spoon in oil, a pinch of salt and about 3/4 cup of water at the end.

RECOMMENDED WINE
MÁDI
Furmint, 2011

PEAR CAKE WITH CHOCOLATE

INGREDIENTS (FOR 4 PERSONS):

FOR THE BASE:

4.5 oz / 125 g milk cocholate (40%)
4.5 oz / 125 g feulletine
4 oz / 110 g cracknel

FOR THE FILLING:

1.5 tbsps / 20 g butter
2 tbsps / 20 g sugar
2 pears, peeled

FOR THE CHOCHOLATE FILLING:

3 oz / 85 g sugar
2 egg yolks
1 oz / 30 g egg (cca. half egg)
4.5 oz / 135 g cocholate (70%)
1 2/3 cups / 165 g heavy cream

FOR THE CHOCOLATE COAT:

1 oz / 20 g chocolate (70%)
1/2 cup / 125 g water
1/4 cup / 60 g heavy cream
1/4 cup / 50 g sugar
1 oz / 2 g gelatin leaf

FOR THE DECORATION:

1/2 cup / 100 g isomalt
edible petals

Melt chocolate and blend with feulletines and grinded cracknels. Pour onto a flat surface and cool. Cut as big round of it as wide you want your cake will be.

Melt butter in a pan and add sugar. Caramelize. When it is golden brown add diced pear. Toss and let cool in the pan. Melt chocolate and set aside. Mix sugar with 1 tbsp water and heat to 250°F (121°C). If you drop sugar of that temperature to ice cold water, it forms a small, soft ball which explodes into tiny drops. Beat lightly egg and egg yolks over a pot of boiling water. Add sugar and stir until cool. Blend with melted chocholate. Whip cream until it forms soft peaks and blend with chocolate mixture. Be quick in order to avoid the collapse of the whipped cream. Place cake base on the bottom of a cake ring. Fill the ring half full of cream. Spread with pear then fill the ring full of cream.

Mix all ingredients except gelatine and reduce by boiling. Remove from heat and add soaked and squeezed gelantin leaf. Cool. Remove ring from cake and transfer on a rack. Pour coating on it and cool. Melt isomalt at 240°F (117°C) without stirring. Cool a bit then make thin strands of isomalt on a baking sheet with a whisk. Be quick. Before set totally, form bird's nest with the petals. Place on the cake right before serving.

ZOLTÁN VIDÁK

RÓKUSFALVY INN

Unlike so many chefs, Zoltán Vidák remembers exactly the moment he decided to be a cook while watching television programme presented by a ship's cook. He has climbed the ladder of success both in Hungary and abroad. His goal has always been to produce the best food from the best ingredients for an appreciative public. This has been successful, as he lives in Etvek where he grows his own vegetables. The locals welcome his food and it has even been enjoyed by movie stars working in the Etyek film studio.

'After borders were opened, Hungarian cuisine was still searching for its way. It was underdeveloped. During training, we only received some tips and knowledge wasn't great but this is being turned around by cooks using new techniques. Fortunately there are several Hungarian cooks worth paying attention to, Lajos Takács and Lajos Bíró for example whose determination has put them in the forefront of Hungarian cookery and from them, I've learned a lot. Generally speaking, I prefer seasonal products but I also love working with rabbit, offal, duck and forest mushrooms. I like Mangalitsa, which tastes good with a creamy consistency. I hope it continues to enjoy popularity and becomes even more successful.'

SIMMERED PORK BELLY WITH CHANTERELLE SALAD

INGREDIENTS (FOR 4 PERSONS):
FOR THE PORK BELLY:
14 oz / 400 g pork belly (1-inch thick)
half bunch of mint
2-3 cloves of garlic
1 tbsp salt
freshly ground black pepper

FOR THE SALAD:
14 oz / 400 g chanterelle, small
2-3 shallots
1 carrot, sliced
3 common juniper seeds
2 bay leaves, whole
1/2 cup / 0.1 l wine vinegar
salt and sugar to taste

FOR THE KOHLRABI:
1 kohlrabi
1 potato
1 onion, finely chopped
1/2 cup / 0.1 l heavy cream
1/4 cup / 50 g butter

Crush garlic. Form a prism from pork belly. Spread with minced mint. Flavor with garlic, salt, pepper and roll up tight. Place into an elastic net, wrap in foil tight and put into a vacuum bag. Bake in water bath at 165°F (75°C) for 20 hours. Transfer to ice cold water then put in the refrigerator for 24 hours. Cut slices with a slicing machine.

Cut onions into thin radial slices. Slice carrots, crush common juniper seeds. Bring a pot of water to a boil then add all spices and chopped vegetables. Boil for a few minutes then remove from heat. Flavors will penetrate chanterelle.

Cut all vegetables into cubes of the same size and cook them in salty water. Drain. Purée vegetables in a blender with cream, butter and cooking water (if needed). Cool.

Serving: Cut paper-thin slices from pork belly. Garnish with salad and kohlrabi purée. Pour some olive oil on it. May be decorated with pigweed and fennel.

RECOMMENDED WINE
ETYEKI KÚRIA
Sauvignon Blanc

MANGALITSA JOWL STEW WITH PORCINI AND CURD CHEESE DUMPLINGS

INGREDIENTS (FOR 4 PERSONS):
FOR THE MARINADE:
10.5 oz / 300 g porcini, small
8-10 cherry tomatoes
2 cups / 0.5 l calf stock
2 cups / 0.5 l red wine
1 tsp red paprika powder
2 oz / 50 g duck fat

FOR THE STEW:
8 Mangalitsa jowls
1 fennel, thin sliced
2 onions, finely chopped
2 tomatoes, peeled
2 capia sweet peppers
1 bell pepper
1 parsley root, thin sliced
3-4 lovage leaves or celery leaves
10.5 oz / 300 g porcini, small
8-10 cherry tomatoes
2 cups / 0.5 l calf stock
2 cups / 0.5 l red wine
1 tsp red paprika powder
2 oz / 50 g duck fat

FOR THE DUMPLINGS:
2 1/2 cups / 300 g flour
3.5 oz / 100 g curd cheese
2 tbsps sour cream
1 egg
2 tbsps chive, minced
parsley oil

Rub Mangalitsa jowls with crushed garlic, black pepper, caraway seeds, thyme, minced chili and oil. Arrange in a plastic box and close hermetically. Put in the refrigerator for 24 hours.

Sear jowls on duck fat the follow-up day. Chop onions finely, cut fennel and parsley root into thin slices. Peel tomatoes. Bake peppers at the highest temperature until their skin turns black. Cool covered. When cool, peel and remove cores. Remove jowls from fat and set aside. Sauté onion, fennel and parsley root on fat. Purée tomatoes and peppers in a blender and add to onions. Cover with stock and wine, bring to a boil. Place Mangalitsa jowls back with lovage or celery leaves. Simmer over very low heat (at 160-175°F) (70-80°C) for 3 hours. Add stock and wine if needed. Peel porcinis. If you cut off a piece, throw it in the stew. When stew is done remove meats and drain gravy. Flavor to taste or add some liquid if needed. Pour back in the pan and bring to a boil together with the meat, porcini and peeled cherry tomatoes.

Combine all ingredients and cut small lumps. Cook in boiling salty water.

Serving: Place dumplings by stew and pour some parsley oil on it.

LIVER SAUTÉ WITH POTATO
AND BAKED ONION

INGREDIENTS (FOR 4 PERSONS):
FOR THE LIVER:

22 oz / 600 g Mangalitsa liver
2 shallots or purple onions
2 capia sweet peppers
1 bell pepper, white
3/4 cup / 0.2 l calf stock, dark
2/3 cup / 0.15 l sunflower oil
1/4 cup / 50 g butter
salt
black pepper
marjoram to taste

FOR THE POTATOES:

4-8 new potatoes
2 tbsps sunflower oil
1/4 cup / 50 g butter
salt
black pepper
marjoram to taste
8-10 spring onions

Cut shallots or purple onions into thin radial slices and sauté on oil, over low heat. Flavor with marjoram, salt and sugar. Bake peppers at the highest temperature in oven until their skin turns black. Put them in a plastic box, close hermetically and cool. Peel and cut into strands. Boil the juice of peppers with calf stock, butter and the leftover baked pepper pieces (if any). Purée in a blender then drain and cool.

Trim membranes from liver and cut into thin slices, or ask the butcher to do it. Stuff liver slices with peppers and onions. Roll up tight. Brush with olive oil and wrap in plastic foil. Place in vacuum bag (you can use shrink wrap as well) and bake in water bath at 140°F for 15 minutes.

Wash potatoes thoroughly. Do not peel. Sprinkle with salt and place in a baking pan. Bake in oven at 445°F for 20 minutes with air circulation until tender. Press down a bit to open them. Place marjoram, grounded black pepper and butter in the center. Put back to the oven and bake until golden brown.

Unwrap liver. Rinse spring onions under cold tap water and remove any wilted or damaged tops or slimy skins on the white parts. Trim off the stringy root. Place them in a pan. Add liver and sear with spring onions until golden brown. Serving: Cut liver into rings and place on a plate decoratively. Pour dripping on it and garnish with potatoes and onions. Sprinkle with salt.

ANDRÁS WOLF

NEW YORK CAFÉ - SALON RESTAURANT

András Wolf took on huge responsability when he became the executive chef of the historical Boscolo New York Palace. He is in charge of every dish prepared in that beautiful building, from breakfast for the hotel guests to their sumptuous dinner, from the cold buffet of conferences to the sweets in the café. Despite this pressure András Wolf adores his job with passion.

'I am a perfectionist in all things. Values of past and present learned from my home are very important to me but my inspiration comes from my desire for perfection and permanent self-criticism. Harmony is very important in food and I'm not happy until colors, look and taste all blend. I have known Mangalitsa for a long time. It is often known from countries where quality ham is produced but I'm delighted with its new popularity in Hungary. But we still have a lot to do for it to develop.'

VARIATIONS ON BEETROOT WITH GOAT CHEESE

INGREDIENTS (FOR 4 PERSONS):

FOR BEETROOT PURÉES:
11 oz / 300 g beetroot, yellow
11 oz / 300 g beetroot, purple
1/2-2/3 cup / 0.1-0.15 l vegetable stock
salt, ground white pepper to taste

FOR THE BEETROOT CHIPS:
7 oz / 200 g beetroot, purple
1/2 cup / 90 g sugar
1 1/4 cups / 0.3 l water

FOR THE BEETROOT MOUSSE:
14 oz / 400 g beetroot, purple
3/4 cups / 0.2 l water
Emulzoon (emulsifier) or soy lecithin
salt and sugar to taste

FOR THE ZUCCHINI MOUSSE:
43 oz / 1.2 kg zucchini
2 cloves of garlic, thin sliced
2/3 cup / 0.15 l heavy cream

FOR THE SERVING:
4 baby beetroots
4 aged goat cheeses, small
3.5 oz / 100 g Mangalitsa bacon, sliced

Cook beetroots in boiling salty water until almost tender. Cook different colors separately. Peel (when still warm) and purée in a blender (still separately). Flavor with salt and ground white pepper. Add some cooking water but not too much, purées must remain thick.

Make a syrup of sugar and water. Peel raw beetroots and cut into paper-thin slices. Scald beetroot slices with boiling syrup. Place them between two silicone sheets and dry.

Dice peeled beetroot. Purée in a blender with salt, sugar and cover with water. Sieve. Add Emulzoon or soy lecithin. Make it foamy with a stick mixer.

Remove core of zucchini and cut into slices. Blanch and refresh. Drain and squeeze water out of it. Boil cream, add garlic and cook for 1 minute. Add to the cold zucchini. Purée in a blender. Flavor with salt. Sieve more times. Drain if it is too watery.

Serving: Cook baby beetroots in salty water until tender. Peel. Place bacon slices on plate. Garnish with beetroot purées, mousses and goat cheese.

RECOMMENDED WINE
2HA WINERY AND WINE CELLAR
Pinot Gris, 2008

MANGALITSA IN PIQUANT VEGETABLE SAUCE WITH LIVER DUMPLINGS

INGREDIENTS (FOR 4 PERSONS):

FOR THE PIQUANT SAUCE:
5.5 oz / 150 g onion
18 oz / 500 g mixed vegetables
(2/3 of them must be carrot)
2 bay leaves, 1 lemon, sliced, 2 oz / 50 g mustard
1/4 cup / 50 g sugar, 7 oz / 200 g sour cream
3/4 cup / 0.2 l extra virgin olive oil
1 1/4 cups / 0.3 l vegetable stock

FOR THE LIVER DUMPLING:
18 oz / 500 g Mangalitsa liver
2 oz / 50 g salvia, 2 eggs
3.5 oz / 100 g Panko breadcrumbs
2 cups / 0.5 l sunflower oil
freshly ground black pepper

FOR THE DUMPLING AND KIDNEY:
36 oz / 1 kg potato, yellow
1-1 1/4 cup / 100-150 g flour
3 egg yolks, 2 cups / 0.5 l sunflower oil
10.5 oz / 300 g Mangalitsa kidney (trimmed)

FOR THE BACON:
29 oz / 800 g Mangalitsa bacon
36 oz / 1 kg Mangalitsa lard
5 cloves of garlic, 1 bell pepper
1 tomato, 2 bay leaves
1 onion, finely chopped

FOR THE JUS:
180 oz / 5 kg Mangalitsa bones (with meat)
54 oz / 1.5 kg mixed vegetables,
half star anise
thyme to taste,
black pepper
bay leaf, 1/4 cup / 50 g butter

Peel vegetables and chop finely. Sauté on oil, add bay leaves, lemon slices, mustard and sugar. Pour some vegetable stock but do not cover. Bring to boil then add some stock. Bring to a boil again. Repeat process until well cooked. Thicken with sour cream. Drain then purée in a blender.

Trim liver from membranes and place in a vacuum bag. Sprinkle with salvia and ground pepper. Bake at 120°F (50°C) for 25 minutes. Purée in a blender when cool enough to handle. Flavor to taste. Spoon in bonbon molds then frost them in the deep-freeze. Dredge frosted bonbons in egg wash and Panko breadcrumbs then fry in deep fat. Cook potatoes. Peel and mash (still warm) and cool. Mix with egg yolks, flavor with salt. Add as much flour as necessary to ensure the dough is not sticking. Form small lumps and parboil them in boiling water. Refresh. Fry them in deep fat. Soak kidneys in ice cold water then cut into strands. Sear on shallow fat (it takes only some seconds). Heat Mangalitsa lard, add spices and slices vegetables. Sprinkle bacon with salt and confit it at 210°F (100°C) for 6 hours. Press down and cool. Slice. Fry on shallow fat until bacon skin is crunchy and all sides are golden brown.

Bake bones in oven at 425°F (220°C) for 230 minutes. Put them into a pot and cover with cold water. Bring to a boil and skim off the scump. Roast vegetables and spices in the oven at 425°F for 10 minutes then add them to the baked bones. Cook for 1.5-2 hours. Drain then simmer it until gets dark, oily liquid. Skim off the scump time to time. Thicken with cold butter before serving.

RECOMMENDED WINE
TOKAJ OREMUS
Mandolás Furmint, 2010

CURD CHEESE PIE WITH APRICOT ICE CREAM AND PÁLINKA MOUSSE

INGREDIENTS (FOR 4 PERSONS):

FOR THE CURD CHEESE PIE:

18 oz / 500 g curd cheese
1/2 cup / 100 g sugar
1 lemon zest
half of Vanilla bean
1 oz / 30 g starch
3 eggs

FOR THE PÁLINKA MOUSSE:

1 cup / 0.25 l water
2/3 cup / 125 g sugar
2 tbsps / 30 ml apricot pálinka (fruit brandy)
4 tbsps Xanthazoon or soy lecithine

FOR THE APRICOT ICE CREAM:

2/3 cup / 0.15 l apricot juice
2/3 cup / 0.15 l water
1/2 cup / 100 g sugar
1 oz / 12 g pectin
21.5 oz / 600 g apricot purée
(or purée made from 36 oz / 1 kg peeled apricot)

FOR THE CRUMBS:

1 cup / 120 g flour
1/4 cup / 60 g butter
1/3 cup / 30 g icing sugar
1 tsp / 10 g salt
1 Vanilla bean

Sieve curd cheese. Add lemon zest, seeds of Vanilla bean, starch, egg yolks and half of the sugar. Whip egg whites until stiff with the other half of sugar. Mix lightly with curd cheese mousse. Dust some sugar in buttered baking molds. Spoon mousse into molds until they fill till 2/3. Bake in oven at 355°F (180°C) for 12 minutes.

Boil water and sugar, thicken with Xanthazoon or soy lecithine. Cool. Add pálinka and pour in a whipping siphon. Charge two cartridges.

Combine all ingredients and boil. Cool. Put it into the deep-freeze and beat it with a whisk in every 15 minutes until we can form it with a spoon. May be made in an ice cream maker as well.

Mix all ingredients well and put in the refrigerator for 24 hours. Roll pastry to 1/5-inch thickness. Bake in oven at 355°F (180°C) for 10 minutes. Cool. Flake and go on baking at 355°F (180°C) until golden brown.

Serving: Place crumbs on plate and put pie and ice cream on it. Spoon some apricot jam in a small glass and press some pálinka mousse on the top.

RECOMMENDED WINE
ROYAL TOKAJI
Áts Cuvée, 2009

KORNÉL ZVEKÁN

ARANYSZARVAS BISTRO

'A food is perfect when it is the No. 1. in the statistics' - states Kornél Zvekán. 'It is so awkward when I find a perfect dish but nobody wants to eat it'. He is blunt and honest, just like his kitchen, where he takes simple, everyday dishes and creates unforgettable culinary dreams from them. He work at the Aranyszarvas Bistro, a restaurant which has a history going back more than 200 years. Tradition and evolution are side by side here since the re-opening of the restaurant.

'I don't like when food is presented on the plate in a very fancy way. What I do like is to present foods of different tastes and consistencies on the same plate. It gives me the opportunity to experiment with ingredients, spices and textures, using seasonal produce to the standard of the restaurant and the pleasure of the guests. I love using Hungarian produce even though the quality isn't always consistent. We work with a lot of game and that is why I cook pheasant soup here. We often offer Mangalitsa and foreigners are surprised that it is a traditional Hungarian pig, so regard it as a rarity and enjoy eating it. We have a lot of work to do the message about Mangalitsa out there but it isn't an impossible task.'

PHEASANT CONSOMMÉ

INGREDIENTS (FOR 4 PERSONS):
2 pheasants (90-108 oz / 2.5-3 kg in total)
18 oz / 500 g carrot, finely chopped
18 oz / 500 g parsley root, finely chopped
18 oz / 500 g onion, finely chopped
1 bunch of parsley, finely chopped
1 blanched celery, finely chopped
1 kohlrabi, small, finely chopped
1/2 celery root, finely chopped
5 sprigs thyme
1 tbsp black pepper seed, whole
half tbsp common juniper
1 Tbsp sea salt, grained
2 oz / 50 g duck fat

Preheat oven to 430°F (220°C). Rinse and prepare the whole pheasants. Remove breasts and thighs. Transfer meats in a baking pan and bake in oven for 25 minutes until golden brown. Place pheasants in a large pot and cover with 14-16 cups of water. Add some salt and bring to a boil. Skim off the scump. Add vegetables and simmer. Remove breasts and thighs one hour later and transfer them in a baking pan. Cover with duck fat. Confit at 210°F (100°C) until meat falls off the bones (it can take some hours). Remove bones when cool enough to handle. Place meat in a terrine mold (to 1-inch thickness). Press down and put in the refrigerator.

Flavor soup with salt to taste and cook for 3.5-4 hours. Remove from flame and let it rest. Drain. Serving: Put a slice of pressed pheasant meat and ladle soup on it. You may add some chopped vegetables as well.

RECOMMENDED WINE
SZÁSZI WINE CELLAR
Badacsonyi Kéknyelű, 2010

MANGALITSA CARPACCIO
WITH FERMENTED PICKLES REMOULADE
AND PAPRIKA KALÁCS

INGREDIENTS (FOR 4 PERSONS):
FOR THE CARPACCIO:
28 oz / 800 g Mangalitsa tenderloin
(in one piece if possible)
salt, freshly ground black pepper to taste

FOR THE REMOULADE:
14 oz / 200 g fermented pickles and their juice
1 bunch of parsley, finely chopped
2 oz / 50 g caper berry, finely chopped
2 quail eggs
3/4 cup / 0.2 l extra virgin olive oil
salt, freshly ground black pepper to taste

FOR THE PAPRIKA KALÁCS
Hungarian sweet bread, very similar to brioche):
1/2 cup / 100 g brown sugar
3.5 oz / 100 g red paprika powder
1 cup / 0.25 l milk
3 1/3 cups / 400 g flour
2 tbsps Mangalitsa lard
1 oz / 25 g yeast
2 Tbsps sour cream

Trim membranes from tenderloin. Rub with salt and pepper. Sear on all sides and put in the refrigerator (still warm). Wrap in plastic foil when cool and place in the deep-freeze.

Mix all ingredients except quail eggs. Sprinkle with salt and pepper. It is recommended to prepare it the day before, flavors have time to mix together. Boil quail eggs and cut into halves.

Preheat oven to 355°F (180°C). Sift flour into a bowl. Warm up milk to room-temperature and put chopped yeast in it. When yeast has risen add to flour. Combine well with sour cream and lard. Let it rise at a lukewarm place for 15-20 minutes then roll out on a floured surface to about a thickness of a finger. Mix red paprika powder with sugar and dust dough with it. Roll up and transfer in a baking pan lined with grease-proof paper. Bake for 20-25 minutes until golden brown. Cool and slice.

Cut tenderloin into paper-thin slices and serve with remoulade, quail eggs and kalács.

RECOMMENDED WINE
GÁL WINERY
Pinot Noir Rosé, 2013

MANGALITSA SPARE RIB WITH MASHED POTATOES, ONION AND SPINACH

INGREDIENTS (FOR 4 PERSONS):
FOR THE SPARE RIB:
36 oz / 1 kg Mangalitsa chuck
2 sprigs thyme
2 bay leaves
8 black pepper seeds, whole
salt, black pepper to taste

FOR THE POTATOES:
36 oz / 1 kg potatoes
1 cup / 100 g corn starch
10.5 oz / 300 g onion, minced
2 oz / 50 g duck fat
salt, black pepper to taste

FOR THE SPINACH:
16 oz / 450 g spinach
3 tbsps olive oil
salt, black pepper to taste

Trim fat from chuck. Sprinkle with salt, place thyme, bay leaves and black pepper seeds next to meat and wrap in plastic foil. Bake in oven with air circulation at 150°F for 15 hours.

Wash potatoes thoroughly and bake them at 285°F for 35-40 minutes until tender. Sauté onion on duck fat. Peel potatoes (still warm) and mash. Add onion. Blend well with salt, pepper and corn starch. Pat in a baking pan to 3-inch thickness. Bake in oven at 285°F for 90 minutes to doneness. Cut in slices and fry in shallow fat before serving.

Stem and wash spinach leaves. Sauté on olive oil. Sprinkle with salt and pepper right before serving. Place chuck slices on plates and garnish with potatoes and spinach.

RECOMMENDED WINE
DÁVID WINE HOUSE
*Dávid Kedvence Kékfrankos Válogatás
(Dávid's Favorite Blaufränkisch Selection),
2009*

RESTAURANTS
IN BUDAPEST

PEST

DUNA

*VI*th distr.

*VII*th distr.

② 17 ② 24

② 2

① 1 ② 6

② 9 ② 7

② 5 ② 16 ② 21

*1*st distr.

② 11

*V*th distr. *VIII*th distr.

DUNA

BUDA

RESTAURANTS
IN THE
COUNTRYSIDE

4 Encs

Tarcal **3**

Esztergom **18** **20** Budakalász

Perbál **23**

Budapest

Etyek **15**

19

Debrecen
12

22
Hajdáböszörmény

8
Veszprém

14 Hévíz

13
Balatonszemes

10
Kecskemét

LIST OF RESTAURANTS

21 HUNGARIAN KITCHEN
Chef: Zsolt Litauszki
21 Fortuna street,
Budapest, H-1014
Phone: +36 (1) 202 2113
www.21restaurant.hu

ALABÁRDOS
Ched: Attila Bicsár
2 Országház street,
Budapest, H-1014
Phone: +36 (1) 356 0851
www.alabardos.hu

**ANDRÁSSY RESIDENCY
WINE & SPA*****
Chef: Ferenc Balázs
94 Fő street,
Tarcal, H-3915
Phone: +36 (47) 580 015
www.andrassyrezidencia.hu

ANYUKÁM MONDTA
Chef: Szabolcs Dudás
57 Petőfi street,
Encs, H-3860
Phone: +36 (46) 587 340
www.anyukammondta.hu

ASTORIA – MIRROR CAFÉ
Chef: Péter Várvízi
19-21 Kossuth Lajos street,
Budapest, H-1051
Phone: +36 (1) 889 6022
www.mirrorcafe.hu

BABEL
Chef: György Lőrincz
2 Piarista köz,
Budapest, H-1052
Phone: +36 (70) 600 0800
www.babel-budapest.hu

BOCK BISTRO
Chef: Lajos Bíró
43-49 Erzsébet road,
Budapest, H-1073
Phone: +36 (1) 321 0340
www.bockbistro.hu

CHIANTI RESTAURANT
Chef: Krisztián Nagy
13 Csermák Antal street,
Veszprém, H-8200
Phone: +36 (88) 410 385
www.chiantietterem.hu

CSALOGÁNY26
Chef: Balázs Pethő
26 Csalogány street,
Budapest H-1015
Phone: +36 (1) 201 7892
www.csalogany26.hu

**FOUR POINTS BY SHERATON
KECSKEMET HOTEL
& CONFERENCE CENTER**
Chef: László Bodócs
6 Izsáki road,
Kecskemét, H-6000
Phone: +36 76 888 500
www.fourpointskecskemet.hu

GOLDEN DEER BISTRO
Chef: Kornél Zvekán
1 Szarvas square,
Budapest, H-1013
Phone: +36 (1) 375 6451
www.aranyszarvas.hu

**IKON RESTAURANT
& LOUNGE**
Chef: Péter Pataky
23 Piac street,
Debrecen, H- 4025
Phone: +36 (30) 555 7766
www.ikonrestaurant.com

KISTÜCSÖK
Chef: László Jahni
25 Bajcsy-Zsilinszky street,
Balatonszemes, H-8636
Phone: +36 (84) 360 133
www.kistucsok.hu

**LOTUS THERME
HOTEL & SPA**
Chef: Attila Tatár
1 Lótuszvirág street,
Hévíz, H - 8380
Phone:+36 83 500 500
www.lotustherme.net

**MANGA RESTAURANT -
HERNYÁK ESTATE**
Chef: László Ruprecht
2684 Öreghegy Présházak,
Etyek, H-2091
Phone: +36 (30) 274 8994
www.hernyak.hu

**NEW YORK CAFÉ -
SALON RESTAURANT**
Chef: András Wolf
9-11 Erzsébet road,
Budapest, H-1073
Phone: +36 (1) 886 6167
www.newyorkcafe.hu

LACIPECSENYE
Chef: Lajos Takács
11 Sas street,
Budapest, H-1051
Phone: +36 70 370 7474
www.lacipecsenye.eu

PRÍMÁS PINCE
Chef: Tibor Jászai
4 Szent István square,
Esztergom, H-2500
Phone: +36 (33) 541 965
www.primaspince.hu

RÓKUSFALVY INN
Chef: Zoltán Vidák
4 Alcsúti street,
Etyek, H-2091
Phone: +36 (22) 597 097
www.rokusfalvyfogado.hu

**SCHIESZL RESTAURANT
AND WINEYARD**
Owner: Konrád Schieszl
Chef: Salamon Tamás
83 Budai street,
Budakalász, H-2011
Phone: +36 26 340 465
www.schieszl.hu/en/

SALON RESTAURANT
Chef: Antonio Fekete
9-11 Erzsébet road,
Budapest, H-1073
Phone: +36 (1) 886 6167
www.salonrestaurant.hu

TUBA FARM
Owner: István Rápolthy
19 Kinizsi Street,
Hajdúszoboszló, H-4200
English speaking contact:
Edit Rapolthy + 36 30 456 88 39
www.tubatanya.hu

WALTER RESTAURANT
Chef: Zoltán Sovák
26 Fő street,
Perbál, H-2074
Phone: +36 (26) 570 007
www.waltervendeglo.hu

WINEKITCHEN
Chef: Ákos Sárközi
3 Sas street,
Budapest, H-1051
Phone: +36 (1) 266 0835
www.borkonyha.hu

⊛

BEREZNAY TAMÁS CHEF
Boook Publishing
tamas.bereznay@boook.hu
www.boook.hu

NOTES

NOTES

FOUR POINTS
BY SHERATON

Kecskemét Hotel
& Conference Center

**Four Points by Sheraton Kecskemét
Hotel & Conference Center**

6. Izsáki Street
Kecskemét, 6000
Hungary

T 0036 76 888 500   **F** 0036 76 888 501
Email sales@fourpointskecskemet.com

ALWAYS A
GREAT STAY

**Everything you need, plus the
style and extras you love.
That's Four Points by Sheraton
Kecskemét Hotel & Conference Center.**

Get what you're looking for with the style and service you want,
all at a great price. We have what matters most to you
like a comfortable bed, a delicious breakfast and fresh coffee.
You'll also find free Internet, free bottled water in your room,
great local beer with Best Brews™ and much more. Whether you're
in town for work or just for fun, you're in for a great stay with us.

Our hotel is in one of the best spots in town, too.
Step out for great local shopping, sports, museums and more.
We're just minutes from the city's historic downtown and
financial center. Plus, a short walk takes you to our
Conference Center. And we're conveniently located near
major highways and offer shuttle service to the
Budapest Liszt Ferenc International Airport every half hour.

Delicious meals

Start your day with breakfast and end it with delicious Hungarian
and International cuisine at our BISTORANT restaurant.
Relax in the Lobby Bar for light snacks and a local craft beer.
In-room dining is also available.

GREAT HOTELS. GREAT RATES.

FOURPOINTS.COM/KECSKEMET

WINKLER WOOLY PIGS

www.WinklerWoolyPigs.com

Learn more about our 5 different boar lineages from original Austrian stock

Sustainably raised accorn finished Mangalitsa pork

Sustainably raised Mangalitsa pork in the heart of Wine Country

Commited to genetically developing this rare heritage breed

WINKLER WOOLY PIGS

(707) 291-5001

Windsor, California

PUREmangalitsa

From the great plains of Hungary,
selected Mangalitsa breeding stock,
registered blood lines,
now available in North America

Please visit us
at **www.puremangalitsa.com**